TRUMP

I'll be your

President

DAVID AGAM

Table of content

As much as you pray to god, god is also praying for you

Introduction

For years, we were told that Republican representatives would stand and fight just as soon as we win a majority in the Senate. Now we are told that we must wait until we will have a Republican President.

This explains the massive frustration with Washington. The American people do not believe Republicans will actually do what they are supposed to do. Despite historic victories handed to the Republicans, the GOP refuse to do what they campaign for and they all become "Campaign Conservatives," and a rubber stamp for Obama's policies. The distaste of Republican voters for politicians who refuse to do their job ended as Trump appeared in the political arena.

Poll after poll this election cycle has registered that voters prefer an outsider with a fresh approach.

When Trump announced his candidacy in June and launched his campaign, many Republicans were nervous. Many of the GOP's members found themselves in a face-off with the voters.

Once in a lifetime a man appears who can capture victories for the public. Trump has done something the Republicans have not done for years. Above all, He speaks the truth. He names them and shames them. Trump is already defying the laws of politics.

Trump has sustained a lead in the polls long before voting will begin, and remains at the top of the polls. Unless tamed, he will win the Presidency.

While they all are preparing to be in the Oval Office, without knowing what to do when they get there, Trump has already written the blueprint of his Presidency.

Donald Trump is larger than life.

Everything he touches turns to gold.

DONALD TRUMP

The sky rumbled. A helicopter appeared, first as a black speck in the clouds, and when it hovered low enough above ground, people could read the letters decorating the side, TRUMP. Everywhere people pointed to the sky and shouted. "Trump! Trump!"

The Sikorsky helicopter landed in parking lot nearby, tossing gravel and dirt into the reporters' faces as they watch the landing. Trump emerges wearing a white and red leather baseball cap that reads "Make America Great, Again".

For decades, presidential contenders have been coming to Iowa to eat hotdogs and greet the farmers, but no one has ever seen anything quite like the fire that sparked when Trump appeared.

Laughing and reaching out to people that were moving forward to shake his hand or take his photo. They shouted things like "We Love You Donald," and singing "Money, Money, Money, Money" the familiar theme song to The Apprentice.

Since the beginning of his campaign, Trump is leading most major polls.

* * * *

Trump is known to the media as The Donald, a nickname spread after his first wife Ivana Trump, referred to him as such, in an interview.

Donald John Trump was born in 1946 in Queens, New York, the fourth of five children of Frederick and Mary Trump. He was an energetic, assertive child, and his parents sent him to the New York Military Academy at age 13, hoping the discipline of the school would channel his energy in a positive manner. Trump did well at the academy, both socially and in academia, rising as a star athlete and leader of the student body by the time he graduated in 1964. He entered Fordham University and then he was transferred to the Wharton School of Finance at the University of Pennsylvania, from which he graduated in 1968 with a degree in economics.

Donald Trump's father greatly influenced his decision to make a career in real estate development, but his goals were on a much grander scale. As a student, Donald Trump worked with his father and after his graduation from college, he join his father's company, the Trump Organization. In a short period, he was able to finance an expansion of the company's holdings by convincing his father to use loans on equity from their apartment buildings. Yet, since the real estate business at the time was extremely competitive; his profit margins were actually narrow. In 1971, Donald Trump moved his home to Manhattan, where he became familiar with many influential people. Shortly after, Trump became involved in large building projects in Manhattan, by using attractive architectural designs and winning public recognition.

When the Pennsylvania Central Railroad entered into bankruptcy, Trump was able to obtain an option on the railroad's yards on the west side of Manhattan. In 1978, his plans to build apartments proved impractical because of a poor economic environment, in a quick maneuver, Trump switched the property to a convention center, and the city approved it over two other sites.

In 1974, Trump obtained an option on the unprofitable Penn Central's hotels, adjacent to Grand Central Station. Trump worked out a complex deal with the city and renovated the building, constructing a striking new facade of reflective glass designed by architect Der Scutt. A year later, he became partner with the Hyatt Hotel Corporation. When the Grand Hyatt opened in 1980, it was popular and an economic success, making Donald Trump the city's best-known developer.

In 1977, Trump married Ivana and together they had three children: Donald, Jr. (born 1977), Ivanka (born 1981), and Eric (born 1984). After the birth of their first child Donald Trump Jr. in 1978, Ivana Trump became the vice president of design in the Trump Organization, and played a major role in supervising the renovation of the Commodore. The couple divorced in 1992.

Trump became involved in many projects in Manhattan.

In 1979, Trump leased a site on Fifth Avenue adjacent to Tiffany & Company as the location for a monumental $200 million dollar apartment-retail complex designed by Der Scutt. When it opened in 1982, it was named Trump Tower.

The 58-story building featured a 6-story atrium lined with

pink marble and included an 80-foot waterfall. The luxurious building attracted well-known retailers and celebrity renters and brought Trump international recognition.

In 1977, Trump begins investigating the profitability of the gambling business. By 1980, he was able to acquire a piece of property in Atlantic City. With the help of his younger brother, Robert, Donald obtained permits and financing for the gambling casino and bought out the Holiday Inn. By 1986, he renamed the facility Trump Plaza Hotel and Casino. Trump purchased the Hilton Hotels-casino in Atlantic City when they failed to obtain a gambling license and renamed the $320 million complex Trump's Castle. Later, while it was under construction, he was able to acquire the Taj Mahal, which he opened in 1990.

The Barbizon-Plaza Hotel, located on Central Park South, was built at a cost of $10 million. With the onset of the Depression, the hotel management struggled to keep up with the mortgage, but after only two and a half years, the property foreclosed, and sold at the auction in July 1933.

In 1988, Donald Trump acquired the hotel and converted it into a 340-unit condominium known as the Trump-Parc-East. Trump also purchased the adjacent smaller building at Central Park South on the southwest corner of Sixth

Avenue. He then renovated the Barbizon, renaming it Trump Park.

In 1985, Trump purchased 76 acres on the west side of Manhattan for $88 million to build a complex he called Television City, which has a dozen skyscrapers, a mall, and a riverfront park. In 1988, he acquired the Plaza Hotel for $407 million and spent $50 million refurbishing it under the direct supervision of his wife, Ivana.

Located within 20 acres of perfectly landscaped gardens and with ocean views, Mar-a-Lago is truly the crown jewel of Palm Beach and an acknowledged landmark in the National Register of Historic Places. The Mar-a-Lago Club is one of the most highly regarded private clubs in the world. It is a perfect setting for Special Events, Holiday Celebrations, Weddings and Galas.

Trump purchasing this landmark in 1985 and made it a club in 1995. It has 126 rooms, designed to provide the best amenities possible for members. A five minute drive away is the acclaimed Trump International Golf Club in West Palm Beach, Florida one of the most beautiful golf courses.

In 1989 Trump builds a condominium project in West Palm Beach, Florida, and also purchased the Eastern Air Lines Shuttle for $365 million, renaming it the Trump Shuttle. In 1990, Trump flew to Los Angeles to unveil his plan to build a $1 billion dollar commercial and residential project featuring a 125-story office building.

The real estate market declined, plummeting the value of Trump's empire and Trump's net worth plunged from an estimated $1.7 billion to $500 million. The Trump Organization required massive loans to keep it from collapsing. Questions were raised whether the corporation could survive and some observers saw Trump's decline as symbolic to many business's economic hardship.

However, Trump had accomplished the impossible by brilliant maneuvers with his lenders gaining their support for him from a rock bottom of over $900 million. Donald Trump's net worth increases and in 1997, his net worth climbed to $2 billion. Banks and bondholders had lost hundreds of millions of dollars, but opted to restructure his debt to avoid the risk of losing more money in court.

Donald Trump marries Marla Maples after his separation and divorce from his wife, Ivana. The new couple had a daughter two months before their marriage in 1993. Trump filed for divorce from Marla Maples in 1997, which became final in 1999. A prenuptial agreement allocated $2 million to Marla.

In January 2005, Donald Trump marries a third time to Melania Knauss and their son, Barron William Trump, was born in March 2006.

During 2004, Donald Trump began starring in the NBC reality series, The Apprentice that quickly became a hit. In later years, the show began displaying celebrities as contestants under the revised name The Celebrity Apprentice.

In 2006, Trump bought the Menie Estate in Balmedie, Aberdeen Shire, in Scotland, creating a golf resort. In April 2014, Trump purchased the Turnberry Hotel and Golf Resort in Ayrshire, Scotland.

In 2011, after much disappointment with the depressed American Real Estate Market, Trump made a rare incursion into the stock market. He stated that he was not a stock market person. Among the stocks, Trump purchased stocks of Intel, Johnson & Johnson, Bank of America, Citigroup, Caterpillar, and Procter & Gamble. In December 2012, he added shares of Facebook to his portfolio.

Trump has seven grandchildren. He has five grandkids from his son Donald Jr. (Kai Madison, Donald John III, Tristan Milos, Spencer Frederick, and Chloe). In addition, he has Two grandkids from his daughter Ivanka, (Arabella Rose, and Joseph Frederick), and a third child on the way.

In 2012 Trump's flirtation with politics returned when he publicly announced he was considering running for president again. However, his association with the "Birther" movement, a fringe group that faithfully believed President Barack Obama was not born in the United States discredited his reputation politically in varying degrees. Nevertheless, Trump continues to be vocal against President Obama, not only in regards to his place of birth, but also on a variety of his political policies.

Anyone who knows Trump well and follows the years and decades of his fame, knows he is unscripted and unfiltered. Trump has made his aggressive brand of authenticity the centerpiece of the dominating polls. Trump has baffled the Republican establishment and puzzled many journalists with his leap to the front of the field in the race to be the GOP's candidate for the Presidency.

Donald Trump is not what you see on the surface. A master trader, he has always played every angle, bullying or flattering, and then suddenly changes direction in order to gain an advantage. He keeps his true intentions to himself, always a few steps ahead of everyone else. Having entered a new game that calls for seeking attention in a crowded modern day politic, Trump is proving that his skills are priceless.

The Trump Organization owns, operates, develops and invests in real estate around the world.

Beyond his traditional ventures in the real estate, hospitality, and entertainment industries and having carved out a niche for the Trump brand within these industries, Trump has moved on to establish the Trump name and brand in a multitude of other industries and products. Trump has succeeded in marketing the Trump name on numerous products. The list is long and includes the mortgage firm - Trump Financial, Trump Sales and Leasing, Restaurants in Trump Tower and Buffet, Catering, Ice Cream Parlor, and Bar. Trump has an online travel website, a Signature Menswear Collection, Accessories, and Watches, Fragrance, Magazine, Golf, Chocolate, Home Furnishings, a television production company, Real Estate, Books, Model Management, Shuttle, and Trump Steaks. Trump reportedly receives $1.5 million for each one-hour presentation he does for The Learning Annex.

Trump says that his brand is worth about $3 billion. Many developers pay Trump to market their properties and to be the public face for their projects. These portions of Trump's Empire are managed by his children, and by far is the most valuable.

On June 16, 2015, Trump officially announced that he is running.

"I am officially running for President of the United States," Trump said during his announcement at Trump Towers in New York City, "And we are going to make our country great again." He then added with his fearless signature style. "I will be the greatest jobs President that God ever created." Trump succeeded, like no one else, in converting celebrity into profit.

THE TRUMP FAMILY

He was born in the southwestern German town of Kallstadt where his family worked on a vineyard in 1869. He became an entrepreneur and made his first fortune operating boomtown hotels, restaurants and brothels in the Northwestern United States. His name was Frederick Drumpf. Frederick is the father of Fred and John Trump and the grandfather of Donald Trump.

In 1894, he operated a hotel in the mining town of Monte-Cristo, Washington. Four years later, he moved to Bennett, British Columbia, and managed the Arctic Restaurant and Hotel, which offered fine dining and lodging around a sea of tents.

As the demand for hotels and restaurants grew, he built a two-story building in Bennett, British Columbia, during the Klondike Gold Rush. The Arctic House was one of the largest and most decadent restaurants in that region of Klondike, offering fresh fruit and ptarmigan in addition to the staple of horsemeat.

Frederick Drumpf established the White Horse Restaurant and Inn in Whitehorse, Yukon.

In 1901, Frederick sold his investments and used the proceeds to return to Germany. In 1902, Trump returned to Kallstadt to marry his old neighbor Elizabeth Christ and then returned to the United States. He worked as a barber and restaurant manager in Woodhaven, Queens, where his sons Fred and John were born in 1905 and 1907.

In 1918, Frederick Trump died of pneumonia flu pandemic. At the time of his death, he began to invest in real estate development in Queens; his wife and his son Fred would continue his real estate projects under the Elizabeth Trump & Son moniker.

Trump's mother, Mary Anne, was born in 1912 at Tong, off the coast of Scotland. In 1930, she met Fred Trump when she was 18, on a holiday in New York. Fred married Mary Anne and fathered Maryanne, Robert, Elizabeth, Donald, and Fred Jr.

Fred Trump built and operated affordable housing from large buildings of multi-family apartments in New York City, including more than 27,000 low-income multifamily apartments and row houses in Coney Island, Bensonhurst, Sheepshead Bay, Flatbush, and Brighton Beach in Brooklyn and Flushing and Jamaica Estates in Queens.

Fred Trump's estimated assets exceeded $300 million. For six years, he suffered from Alzheimer's disease before his death from pneumonia in June of 1999, and he died at Long Island Jewish Medical Center, in New Hyde Park, New York.

MELANIA TRUMP

Born in Slovenia in 1970 when it was part of Yugoslavia, she's the daughter of an Austrian man named Victor, who managed a chain of car and motorcycle dealerships, and a Slovenian woman who was a fashion designer.

Well-mannered and shy, the teen went on to study architecture and design at the University of Ljubljana and was set on the path to meet The Donald.

The first party she ever came to was the one she met Donald.

She was 28. He was 52. It was love at first sight for Trump, but when the well-known womanizer tried to get Melanie's number, she refused, asking that he give her his instead. Donald gave her all of his numbers business and home — and she called him when she returned from a modeling trip.

Donald was separated from his second wife, Marla Maples. After Melania called him, he was a one-woman man. Seven years later, they married in a lavish, much-publicized ceremony at his Mar-a-Lago resort in Palm Beach Florida. Her Christian Dior dress alone cost $100,000 and had a 13-foot train and a 16-foot bridal veil.

Melania gave birth to Barron William Trump, Trump's fifth child, in 2006.

As a wife to Donald and mother to Barron, she runs her own jewelry business, and in her Eastern European accent successfully sells her jewelry on QVC.

She is the better half — the more low-key, the quiet half of Donald Trump. Friends and acquaintances say she would make a Great First Lady.

Melania seems to be making an impact behind the scenes. Trump confessed that she told him to stop attacking Jeb Bush.

The billionaire real estate mogul is often out and about with his wife by his side. Looking to boost his favorability with women, Trump plans to spotlight his wife and daughter, and their dedication to bring awareness and support for women's health issues and this could help soften the candidate's edges. Asked if they shared his opposition to abortion, Trump demurred. "I'm going to let them reveal themselves if people are going to ask that question, which they might not," he said.

If Donald Trump wins the Presidency, his wife Melania will be the first foreign-born first lady since John Adams' spouse, Louisa.

IVANKA TRUMP

In 2010, she took it to Fox News and calmly criticized President Barack Obama and his "anti-business rhetoric," and stressed that she's "not overly supportive" of the President.

The former model Ivanka, 33, is not in the spotlight as much as her father is. Ivanka's face frequently appeared on the cover of magazines for years, but, unlike her father, Ivanka seems secure about herself and her prominence. As the second-most famous member of the family, Donald Jr. her brother; Ivanka appears to be missing the desperation gene that drives her father's constant pursuit of fame.

However, Ivanka Trump, who grew up playing in her father's office, is his most influential adviser. She was the first person Donald Trump mentioned by name, when he was asked who does he count on the most. Ivanka introduced her father, while his wife, Melania stood by in the background. Ivanka's style is more polished she is softer, and more refined than her father's characteristics of the television character George Jefferson and the movie actor John Wayne. She is the antidote to Trump's abrasiveness. Ivanka is extremely careful with her public statements. She constantly strikes the proper notes when asked about her father, praising his record and avoiding controversies.

She acknowledges that her father turns to her for advice and insists that she would not be where she is now in life if her father did not strongly believe in women's quality and excellence.

Ivanka said that the media had sensationalized the Kelley-Trump mess, and that she was not interested in that. Ivanka Trump never dwells on scandals

"My father is very blunt," she alleged. "When he speaks, he is not gendered specific in his criticism of people." "I'm a businesswoman, not a politician, so I'll leave politics to other members of the family and the many, many people who are involved in the race."

At the campaign events, she almost exclusively speaks about her father's brilliance, passion, work ethic, and his refusal to take 'No' for an answer.

On the rare occasions, when Ivanka has plunged deeper into policy, she has been pro-women and pro-business. She is consistently on-message with her larger-than-life father. When she speaks of him, Ivanka's eyes glance upward. He is The Donald, as their mother Ivana, Trump's ex-wife, called him. Trump hovers like the Goodyear Blimp over the Trump- Organization. In the meantime, each of his children hold the rank of executive vice president in the family business, and are slowly taking command of the different parts of the Empire, which is worth over $10 billion. Ivanka focused her attention to the Trump hotels and her fashion-oriented businesses.

"I wanted to be a businesswoman from as early as I can remember, and my real passion specifically was in Real Estate."

Ivanka has always been the most visible in the family. She is the product of the exclusive Chapin-School in Manhattan and Choate Rosemary Hall in Connecticut. She appeared as a model in 1997 when she was just 16 years old and she showed up in advertisements for Tommy Hilfiger and performed in fashion shows for Versace, Marc Bouwer and

Thierry Mugler. Ivanka's style has always stressed a kind of polished femininity that communicated a self-assurance that her father never mastered.

Ivanka went on to work as a real estate executive in the family firm and started her own shoe, clothing and accessories lines, that are of the luxury category and are popular with working women. On The Apprentice a reality TV show, it became a promotional vehicle for her fashion ventures; and she served as a moderator.

The caution and composure Ivanka brings to business is applied in every corner of her life and is the product of growing up as a child with Trump.

Donald Trump believes that negativity is not a family value, and he generally interprets reality in a way that allows him to appear superior, if not heroic. But Ivanka does not have to win every contest. She can allow that others may be right even in their skepticism; and in contrast to her father's habit of arguing every criticism issue so he comes out on top. Ivanka's Grandfather was a rich man, who shy-away from the public. Ivanka is the daughter of an even wealthier father who seems compelled to mark his name on everything in sight.

Speaking at Fortune's Most Powerful Women Summit in Washington, she is asked whether she is happy her father is running for President.

"I'm incredibly proud of him, it's an incredibly difficult thing to do, as a citizen, and I love what he's doing. As a daughter, it's more complicated."

She said that the level of scrutiny regarding her father's candidacy is beyond what she expected. Donald Trump has ruffled feathers with his off-with- the-head style and his controversial remarks about immigrants, women and his presidential rivals. Yet Ivanka doesn't see that as necessarily a bad thing.

"Whether you disagree or you agree, I think people appreciate the honesty of his dialogue," she said. "And based on his poll numbers, clearly a lot of people do agree with him."

"I think everybody can appreciate the fact that he's creating dialogue," she added.

THE REPUBLICAN NOMINATION PROCESS

Republicans of all stripes thought the unpleasantness of the process has motivated the strongest candidates to sit out of the election in its entirety. The party's base of Conservative Activists believe the process favors candidates with the most money and the views of wealthy donors, and this is damaging to the party's image.

The Republican Party presidential-nomination process is not designed with conservative goals in mind. The Republican Party emulates almost every detail from the Democratic primary process.

Presidential candidates are not accustomed to spending a whole year in Iowa coffee shops and in New Hampshire Town Hall meetings trying to win their parties' nominations. One of the most troublesome aspects of the current process is its gross inefficiency.

The length of the campaign alone keeps many potential candidates on the sidelines. In particular, those in positions of leadership at various levels of our government cannot easily put aside their duties and shift into full-time campaign mode for an extended period of time.

This campaign also requires candidates to spend an excessive amount of time raising money just to compete for the nomination. Generally, only a couple of candidates have sufficient access to such money, and they are joined in the race by those who have essentially no money but are eager for the 15 minutes of fame they receive by sharing a debate stage with legitimate contenders. These low-budget candidates tend to use their newfound notoriety to self-promote or to float their policies. The result is that, before they even run against a Democrat, the ultimate Republican nominee must respond to baseless attacks and marginal philosophies that can discredit the whole party. Many statesmanlike candidates hesitate to run, especially those who do become less statesmanlike in the process.

This process does a poor job of selecting viable presidential contenders. It takes too long and costs too much. It deters good true leaders from running, and the eventual nominee is dragged through the mud for no real purpose.

Since the emergence of the modern primaries, the media has played a decisive role by assigning the candidates' momentum. Most Journalists, are Democrat, who like to influence the result by constantly declaring who is up and who is down. What's more scary, the emergence of an extensive televised debate process has given reporters even greater power. They get to ask questions to the candidates and to referee the arguments amongst themselves, during the only time the candidate's exposure is available to many voters. More often than not, the goal of these journalists is not to inform the Republican Electorate but to create their own storylines by embarrassing candidates or forcing them to answer unrealistic hypothetical questions.

Iowa, New Hampshire, Michigan, and Florida have positioned themselves at the beginning of the primary process, competing to preserve their status as the early deciders, to push the nomination process further and further forward, not because it is good for the country, but because it makes their states more important and gives their voters huge disproportionate influence over our politics.

These state organizations know that the candidates will participate in the primaries however early they are set; and the media will simply extend its coverage, and that these states will continue to enjoy their undue influence as significant.

Candidates for the GOP nomination must rely heavily on campaign consultants. The elite donors have an influence that is disproportionate to their numbers. They hold the positions they do because of their skills of polling, advertising, message formation, and so forth, and not because they necessarily share the views of the broader GOP Electorate.

This has had a significant effect on the winning candidate who often claims victory not so much because he has articulated the values and interests of the party, but because his advertisements managed to sway the late-deciding, independent voters who have little stake in the outcome. If not for Donald Trump and his supporters, who are no longer willing to be co-defendants to their own destitution, find a pathway to defeat the RNC's scheme. The GOP road map to nominate Jeb would never be successful.

Almost unnoticed, the RNC made some changes to the party rules that could make it even harder in 2016. One change in particular could make it virtually impossible for a movement candidate to become the 2016 nominee.

That change is well known as the "proportionality window." It requires all state contests, whether caucuses or primaries, held between March 1 and March 14 to proportionally allocate the delegates available statewide. The states can still allocate delegates available at the congressional-district level by a winner-take-all method.

Only Iowa, New Hampshire, South Carolina, and Nevada are permitted to hold their contests before March 1 without incurring draconian penalties, including reducing a state's delegation to as few as nine. Thus, the combination of these two rules means that the nominee will very likely be whoever wins the contests held after March 14, since it will be impossible to run up a sizeable delegate lead in the early phase of the race when many candidates are competing.

This is a potential death sentence for the conservative candidate. Most of the highly conservative in the southern states are traditionally holding their primaries inside of the March 1–14 window. If that occurs again in 2016, a conservative candidate will probably not gain many delegates over the establishment choice by winning those states. A candidate will then have to compete in less hospitable states that have the freedom to select all of their delegates by winner-take-all methods.

This game is rigged, even for The Donald. The RNC will try one way or another, to make sure one of their own establishment candidate wins the primary. Republican Party bosses like the Koch brothers could rig the secret rules so delegates at the convention vote to keep the nomination from Trump. This process was set up for Bush or Walker to win.

On these primaries, it is all built on a house of cards and fabricated reality. There's hundreds of millions of dollars at stake to buy votes for primary elections. Delegates are not bound to vote for any candidate once the convention opens. The convention is not legally bound by state election results. With so many candidates, it's likely that no one will reach the RNC's required threshold to put their names officially into nomination.

The RNC establishment was not about to turn over control of its convention to Trump as they did in 2012 to Mitt Romney before he was nominated.

Depending on how Trump fares once the 2016 state nominating contests begin, party bosses may find themselves looking at a broken barrel. The GOP establishment also could try to rig new rules to make it harder for Trump. The GOP is the political party that specializes in tilting voting rules to try to shape the outcome. They have done this through adopting dozens of laws, toughening voter ID requirements, limiting early voting, demonizing voter registration drives, etc.

How far the party bosses can push the rules to make it harder for Trump to get the 1,236 delegates needed to secure the nomination? It is clear they can lengthen the distance to the finish line.

The GOP field may see some candidates drop out, but it is likely that a half-dozen or more will keep going, as many of them have billionaires to back them.

The question is whether the RNC could stop a Trump by joining more states into the winner-take-all column. Right now Florida is one of six, winner-take-all states, which Bush is counting on to boost his candidacy. But if Trump holds on above 30 percent or more of the delegates, none of the other candidates have a chance against Trump. In other words, Trump should emerge with the most delegates, even though by itself, it's not enough to secure the nomination. That will assure Trump of getting some significant number of delegates, assuming he hasn't blazed out.

The RNC is a Private Corporation. It does not operate under state law. It is not legally bound to recognize the results of state elections. It does not have any constitution to answer to. Many unforeseen things will happen. If support for Trump continues through this fall, pay attention to how the party bosses may try to tilt the 2016 Caucus, Primary and State Convention rules to impede his path to the nomination.

The serious commentators put Trump in the same league with Reagan. But yet, no one in the media is willing to predict that Trump wins the Republican race, not to mention the elections themselves. The voices of the naysayers is weakening, Trump now leads safely over the 16 competitors. Although this may be an optical illusion; since about 35% of voters support the Republicans at a national level and in states where primaries are held first. But then many are consistently refusing to get carried away to prefer his opponents.

TRUMP TOWER

When Donald Trump built Trump Tower in 1983, it became one of the most recognizable mixed-use skyscrapers in the world, as it is visually striking and very elegant with its sawtooth faceting.

Rising 664 feet above 5th Avenue between East 56th and East 57th streets, Trump Tower was completed in 1983 as the tallest all-glass structure in Manhattan.

Der Scutt, of Swanke, Hayden & Connell, designed the 58-story mixed-use skyscraper. The tower's design was brilliantly executed with nice landscaping hosting vocal performances during the Christmas seasons, and has become the most charming display in The Big Apple famed for its Holiday Celebrations. It's owned and operated by Donald Trump.

Trump Tower significantly reinforced the Plaza District and became the developer's flagship with spectacular views and a 7-story mirrored atrium with waterfall. The mid-tower offices and 256 residential condominiums on the top 38 floors created a new standard of polished and pampered luxury. It is located at the retail epicenter of New York with Tiffany's, Bergdorf Goodman and Louis-Vuitton just a few steps away. The large Fifth Avenue entrance leads to the office elevators and the retail atrium. The entrance to the residences is on East 56th Street. The Fifth Avenue entrance is covered in pink & white-veined marble. This includes the office lobby, the atrium and a pedestrian bridge that crosses over the waterfall's pool. The atrium is crowned with a large, slanted skylight. The 100-foot-high atrium, lined with mirrors creates delightful visual excitement for tourists who ride the crisscrossed escalators to the upper and lower retail floors. At the top level there are very handsome outdoor terraces overlooking to the former IBM Building on the eastern half of the block and adjoining the Nike Store. The architecture permits up to 13 corner rooms per residential floor.

At the top level of the Trump Tower Atrium, there are outdoor terraces overlooking the great atrium of the former IBM Building.

Trump Tower has many amenities including valet, concierge and door attendants, a fitness center, house service, a residents' lounge and a garage. Public restrooms are tucked away on the lower level of the atrium down the south corridor.

In 1998, Trump permitted the Fifth Avenue facade above the entrance to be altered to accommodate a two-story-high sign for "Avon."

Without Trump Tower, the IBM Building and the former AT&T Building across the street might not have been developed.

Trump Tower is the "signature" project of developer Donald Trump. It is triumphant because of its flair and architecture, its location and its views. To his great credit, Trump has remained and maintained his office here as well as occupying the penthouse.

The building acquired new fame as the site of Trump's popular television series, "Celebrity Apprentice."

Trump and his family reside in the three-story penthouse, at the top of the building. "Some people consider it to be the greatest apartment in the world. I would never, ever say that myself, but it's certainly a nice apartment" Trump said.

Sitting atop the 68-story glass skyscraper, the apartment is modeled after the Palace of Versailles; it boasts floor-to-ceiling windows, hand-painted ceilings, fountains, paintings, lots of marble and the crowning glory: two huge gold-plated entrance doors. Real estate experts estimate that if the penthouse would ever come on the market this residential palace would far exceed the current U.S. record of the most highly valued residential property ever to come to market.

No other executive in America, and perhaps the world, could turn something so common, ordinary and insignificant into a landmark of great luxury. There is no other Donald Trump. In his wealth and fame, he is truly a man for our time, the ultimate expression of the American Spirit in the 21st Century.

CARS AND PLANES

Trump's main ride is a Boeing 757, which he purchased in 2011 from Microsoft Co-founder Paul Allen and then upgraded it to Trump standards: Rolls-Royce Engines, 24-Carat-Gold trim and seat-belt buckles, leather seats for up to 43 passengers, TV screens and 2 bedrooms in the space that would normally carry 228 people. It features a dining room, big screen TVs, a master, a guest bedroom, and even a shower. Along the side of the aircraft, the Trump name is prominently displayed.

Among the Donald Trump fleet of aircraft, you could find a large commercial sized plane, a corporate jet and two helicopters. Trump also owns a Cessna Citation X corporate jet designed to seat 12 passengers. The plane is painted in white and features the Trump family crest in gold near the passenger door.

Trump also owns two Sikorsky S-76B helicopters built in 1989 and 1992. Four aircraft is actually a major downsize for Trump who once owned an airline with a fleet of 17 planes.

In 1989, Trump bought Eastern Airline's shuttle service for $380 million dollars and offered frequent flights between cities in the northeast, but encountered economic struggle.

In 1992 Trump Airline defaulted and was taken over by the banks, and later sold to US Air.

The 52-foot executive helicopter seats 12 comfortably - including the pilot. The luxury helicopter's interior has cream-colored Italian-leather seating, with 18-Karat Gold-Plated seat-belt buckles.

＊ ＊ ＊ ＊

Most of the time Trump rides in a limo chauffeured by one of his two New York drivers. It is the very best perk of being rich. When The Donald showed up for jury duty at the New York Superior Court in Manhattan in August, his limo

dropped him directly in front of the court house building and sat in the no stopping zone until he came out hours later.

Trump has a handful of elite foreign cars sprinkled around his various properties, according to his campaign. He's a big fan of Rolls-Royce and in his private collection he began with a vintage 1956 Silver Cloud; now there is a 2015 Rolls-Royce Phantom, as well as a Maybach, a Ferrari, a Cadillac Escalade and a Tesla. There is also a Mercedes-Benz S600 and an SLR McLaren that he bought as a present for Melania. The electric-blue 1997 Lamborghini Diablo he bought was featured in the 2005 episode of "The Apprentice" and the celebrities designed a promotional advertising campaign for the luxury Italian manufacturer.

THE YACHT

The 282-foot Yacht, would be worth $250 million today, and was originally built for Saudi billionaire Adnan Khashoggi in 1980. It was the third-largest yacht in the world at the time, boasting room for 22 passengers and 52 crewmembers, 11 luxury staterooms, 3 elevators, a movie theater, a disco, a swimming pool and a helicopter landing deck. The Yacht is seen in the James Bond movie "Never Say Never Again" as the ship of the villain Maximilian Largo. Khashoggi sold the yacht to the Sultan of Brunei, who sold it to Trump in 1987 for a measly $29 million.

Trump sold the boat to Saudi Prince Al-Waleed, for $20 million and since then he has not purchased another boat.

BANKRUPTCIES

People ask, "How is Donald Trump able to file for bankruptcy so many times?" The answer is "He didn't." Trump himself has never filed for bankruptcy. His corporations have filed for Chapter 11 bankruptcy four times.

Corporations are allowed to continue running while restructuring and reducing their debt. By allowing the business to continue, employees still have their jobs and the business is still making money, corporate debts repaid but may be reduced and must be approved by the creditors and by the bankruptcy court. This is an important distinction when considering Trump's ability to emerge relatively unscathed, at least financially.

A corporation is a separate legal entity from its owners and CEO and it filed for bankruptcy under its own name.

The owners' personal assets are not at risk.

In 1985, Trump opens the Trump Castle after purchasing an unopened Hilton Hotel and getting a second casino license. Harrah files for an injunction to prevent Trump from using his name on the new hotel, saying it will confuse customers but the judge rules in Trump's favor. A year later, Trump bought out Harrah's interest in the Trump Plaza, and became the sole owner of two casinos.

Trump's Taj Mahal located in Atlantic City was in debt for billions of dollars. Trump financed the construction of the Trump Taj Mahal with junk bonds and was unable to pay the high interest. As a result, Trump's corporation filed for Chapter 11 bankruptcy in 1991. The court allowed Trump to reorganize his corporate debts and allowed the casino to keep operating. Trump did surrender half of his ownership interests in the Taj Mahal. To help make loan payments Trump sold his yacht and airplane.

In 1992, Trump owed $550 million on the Trump Plaza Hotel. At this time, Trump filed for Chapter 11 bankruptcy. As part of the restructuring, Trump gave Citibank a 49% interest in the hotel in exchange for a lenient repayment plan. Trump was able to stay on as CEO but he had to give up his salary.

In 2004, Trump Hotels and Casino Resorts Corporation

had $1.8 billion dollars of debt and filed for bankruptcy. Trump reduced his share in the company to 25% thereby, surrendering his control of the corporation and received lower interest rates and another loan to upgrade the properties.

In 2009, Trump Entertainment Resorts filed bankruptcy after missing a large bond interest payment. Trump was not able to agree with his board of directors on a repayment plan so he resigned as Chairman of the board but retained a 10% ownership interest in the corporation.

His business was in the red, and so was he, to the tune of over $900 million in personal debt.

"It was the first bankruptcy and was the only time his personal fortune was at stake," Trump said.

In 2014 Trump Plaza closes, shortly after Trump Entertainment Resorts again files for bankruptcy. Carl Icahn, who holds much of Trump Entertainment's debt, gains control of it and the Taj Mahal.

Icahn reaches an agreement with Trump in 2015 to keep Trump's name on the Trump Taj Mahal Casino after Trump and Ivanka sued seeking to have their name stripped from it. The Taj was going to close down in late 2014, but Icahn is now trying to reorganize and improve it.

BEAUTY PAGEANTS

Donald Trump owned the Miss Universe Organization since 1996 and became a joint partner in 2003 with NBC. The organization produces the Miss Universe, Miss USA, and Miss Teen USA pageants. In December 2006, talk show host Rosie O'Donnell criticized Trump's compassion toward Miss USA, Tara Conner, after she had violated pageant behavioral guidelines. This sparked a tabloid war between the counter puncher, Trump, and O'Donnell, which lasted for several weeks. He appeared on several television shows calling her names, threatening to sue her, threatening to take away her partner Kelli and claimed that Barbara Walters regretted hiring her.

Donald Trump is a two-time Emmy Award–nominated personality, has made appearances as a caricatured version of himself in television series and films like Home Alone 2, Lost in New York, The Nanny, The Fresh Prince of Bel-Air, Days of Our Lives, Wall Street, and as a character in The Little Rascals. More than ever before Trump has been the subject of comedians, Flash cartoon artists, and online caricature artists.

Trump also had his own daily talk show radio program called "Trumped"!

THE APPRENTICE

In 2003, Trump became the executive producer and host of the NBC reality show, The Apprentice, in which a group of competitors battled for a high-level management job in one of Trump's commercial enterprises. The other contestants were successively "fired" and eliminated from the competition. In 2004, Donald Trump filed a trademark application for the catchphrase "You're fired."

For the first year of the show, Trump was paid $50,000 per episode or roughly, $700,000 for the first season, but following the show's success he is currently paid $3 million per episode, making him one of the highest paid TV personalities. In 2007, Trump received a star on the Hollywood Walk of Fame for his many contributions to television.

Trump also put together The Celebrity Apprentice with British TV producer Mark Burnett where well-known stars compete to win money for their own charities. Trump stayed in the forefront while contributing his own money to the various charities.

In February 2015, Trump opted not to renew his television contract for The Apprentice, generating speculation that he might run for President of the United States in 2016.

Roger Stone, a longtime political adviser to Trump until he parted ways with the campaign, argues that television and a unique celebrity persona is central to Trump's success as a presidential candidate.

"Fifteen series of The Apprentice has made Trump a polished television performer," Stone says. "If you look at the show he looks like a decisive, tough leader, in the high-back chair, perfectly lit, perfectly made-up, making decisions."

Stone use to work for Ronald Reagan and recalls how in 1980 a reporter asked the presidential candidate how an actor could occupy the White House. Reagan replied, "How can a president not be an actor?"

"The voters do not always distinguish between reality TV and politics." Stone added.

The 'Celebrity Apprentice' is a more honest show, which

does not pretend to be an imaginary storyline. It had to do with business management. It is about real life competition of real businesses. Donald Trump donated one-fifth to charity.

WORLD WRESTLING

Trump's official relationship with WWE began in 1988 when he hosted WrestleMania IV at his Atlantic City Trump Plaza.

Trump is a known World Wrestling Entertainment fan, and the WWE owner Vince McMahon was his friend. Before Donald Trump was dominating sitting governors and U.S. senators in the polls, the top GOP presidential contender was facing off with Vince McMahon, the CEO of World Wrestling Entertainment.

Trump has hosted two WrestleMania events in the Trump Plaza and has been an active participant in several of the shows. Trump's Taj Mahal in Atlantic City hosted the 1991 WBF Championship owned by WWE. At WrestleMania XX, Jesse Ventura interviewed Trump.

Trump's involvement with pro wrestling goes back more than a quarter of a century. In the beginning, the logic was simple: WWE was staging big events at Trump-owned venues, so he had a stake in promoting this sport. However, over time, Trump was drawn into WWE's staged storylines as a showman, an impresario, a larger-than-life hero; The Donald is in real life what pro wrestlers try to portray themselves as in the ring. It was a match made in promoter heaven. Trump continued to make appearances at various wrestling matches.

Trump and McMahon's relationship takes a turn when his wife Linda McMahon, runs for public office a second time for the U.S. Senate seat in 2012, after her failed run in 2010. While Trump is pushing the Obama "birther" conspiracy; Linda McMahon's campaign attempts to distance itself from The Donald by denying that WWE donated $5 million to Trump's charity in exchange for his WrestleMania appearances.

The tension that moment provoked between the McMahons and Trump was cooled-off by 2013; when Trump was inducted into the WWE Hall of Fame.

LEGAL AFFAIRS

Over the course of his career, Trump has initiated and has been the target of hundreds of civil lawsuits. During the 2008 financial crisis, Trump International Hotel and Tower in Chicago was unable to sell sufficient units. The Deutsche Bank refused to let Trump lower the prices on the units to spur sales. Arguing that the financial crisis and resulting drop in the real estate market is due to circumstances beyond his control, Trump invoked a clause in the contract not to pay the loan. Trump then initiated a suit asserting that his image had been damaged. Both parties agreed to drop their suits.

In 2008, Trump filed a $100 million lawsuit for alleged fraud, and civil rights violations against the city of Rancho

Palos Verdes regarding the golf course purchased by Trump in 2002 for $27 million. The suit was ultimately withdrawn in 2012 with Trump and the city agreeing to modified geological surveys and permit extensions for 20 proposed luxury homes in addition to 36 homes previously approved.

Trump sued comedian Bill Maher for $5 million in 2013, based on comments Maher made on The Tonight Show with Jay Leno, in which Maher offered $5 million payable to a charity if Trump produced his birth certificate to prove his mother had not mated with an orangutan. Trump produced his birth certificate, filing a lawsuit after Maher was not forthcoming, claiming Maher's $5 million offer was legally binding. Trump withdrew his lawsuit against the comedian after eight weeks.

In 2013, a lawsuit filed by the New York Attorney General accused Trump of defrauding more than 5,000 people of $40 million for the opportunity to learn Trump's real estate investment techniques in a for-profit training program. In January 2014, the New York Superior Court upheld part of the Attorney General's case against Trump, and in October 2014, found Trump liable for not obtaining a license to operate the for-profit investment school. In a separate class action civil suit in mid-February 2014, a San Diego federal judge allowed claimants in California, Florida, and New

York to proceed. Trump counterclaimed, alleging that the state Attorney General investigation was dismissed.

In August 2014, a federal judge upheld a $5 million judgment awarded to Donald Trump's Miss Universe Organization after the company successfully sued the ex-Miss Pennsylvania USA for defamation over her claim that the Miss USA pageant was rigged. Trump's lawyer said that Monnin's allegations had cost the pageant a lucrative British Petroleum sponsorship deal and threatened to discourage women from entering Miss USA contests in the future. One can reasonably see that various factors may lead to the final decision in the process. Monnin was not required to retract her original statements.

In 2015, Trump initiated a $100 million's lawsuit against Palm Beach County claiming that officials pressured the FAA to direct air traffic to the Palm Beach International Airport in a "deliberate and malicious" act over his Mar-A-Lago Estate. The air traffic is allegedly damaging the construction of the building and disrupting its ambience.

Trump filed his Statement of Candidacy with the Federal Election Commission. This filing took place well in advance of the July 1 deadline. Donald Trump stood before thousands of supporters to announce his candidacy for President of the United States with his family by his side.

Trump declared his candidacy at Trump Tower where he spoke about the challenges we are currently facing as a nation, his proven record of success, and his belief in the Free Market, a strong military and our country's sacred obligation to take care of our veterans and their families.

"We don't win anymore, whether it's ISIS or whether it's China with our trade agreements. No matter what it is, we don't seem to have it. The nuclear deal with Iran is a disaster. This deal is going to lead to nuclear proliferation. You are going to have nukes; you are going to have countries fighting like hell to get them. Quite simply, it is time to bring real leadership to Washington. The fact is, the American Dream is dead, but if I win, I will bring it back bigger and better and stronger than ever before. Together we will Make America Great Again!"

Trump has teams based in the early primary states of Iowa, New Hampshire and South Carolina. Ivanka Trump officially opened four full-time staffers in New Hampshire and an office based in Manchester.

The New- Hampshire House Representative, Stepanek, who joined Trump's leadership team and works with his campaign to continue to share Trump's messages, was the first to endorse trump. Trump described him as a great addition to his team and was proud to have his endorsement for the Republican Presidential Primary Nomination. He added later that Stepanek understands what is at stake with the economy, and "he will be an asset as we continue to solidify our position at the top of the field, both in New Hampshire and nationally."

Over the past several months, Trump visited New Hampshire, Iowa and other states numerous times. In those events, he gathers the largest crowd in history. Every event has sold out within twelve minutes and has a waiting list of over two thousand people.

TRUMP'S BOOKS

Donald Trump will release a new book.

"The Art of the Deal," published in 1987, it is Trump's first book, and probably his best known.

Trump has written more than 15 books, including "Trump: How to Get Rich," and "Think Big and Kick Ass in Business and Life."

Donald Trump wrote three memoirs, three business-advice titles and two political books, all published between 1987 and 2011.

When Trump talks foreign policy, whether it is economic, diplomatic or military in nature, his positions come soaked in the same baptismal water. His last book on public policy, "Time to Get Tough," appeared in late 2011.

"The fact is, people didn't want to hear from Donald Trump about politics but about business," he wrote. "That's why I wrote 'The Art of the Deal' and many of my other books, they were huge successes. In fact, 'The Art of the Deal' is said to be the biggest-selling business book of all time."

"We don't owe the Middle East any apologies," Trump wrote. "America is not what's wrong with the world. We are an example of freedom to the world. No one can match America. We have big hearts and the courage to do what's right. However, we are not the world's police officers. Moreover, if we have to take on that role, we need to send a clear message that protection comes at a price. If other countries benefit from our armed forces protecting them, those countries should cover the costs. Period."

Trump has a serious beef with China, and how the country uses currency manipulation to game the export market, and believes the United States should threaten China with economic sanctions if it does not set the yuan at a fair market rate.

"Here's the solution: get tough," Trump wrote. "Slap a 25 percent tax on China's products if they don't set a real market value on their currency. End of story. You think the Chinese wouldn't respond constructively. No businessman I know would want to turn his back on the U.S. market — and the Chinese wouldn't either."

"So, I speak badly of China, but I speak the truth and what do the consumers in China want? They want Trump," he wrote. "You know what that means? That means they respect people who tell it like it is and speak the truth, even if that truth may not be so nice towards them."

"So here's the deal: any foreign country shipping goods into the United States pays a 20 percent tax," Trump wrote. "If they want a piece of the American market, they're going to have to pay for it. No more free admission into the biggest show in town and that especially includes China."

When Trump gets into policy specifics, he makes it rather simple, as is his take on income taxes. For instance, he is for eliminating the federal corporate income tax except American companies that outsource jobs to other countries, which would then pay at a rate of 15-20 percent.

Making Mexico pay for Mexicans who entered the country illegally and housed in American jails and prisons.

"I actually have a theory that Mexico is sending their absolute worst, possibly including prisoners, in order for us to bear the cost, both financial and social. This would account for so much crime and violence."

Trump wrote that his wife, Melania, told him that he would

not win a presidential election because, "You're a little wild and a little too controversial. They respect you, they think you are smart, the smartest of all. People really want you. People want you and really need you." This is a great compliment coming from a very smart woman." Trump said.

RELIGION

Trump is a Presbyterian, a member of New York City's Marble Collegiate Church. Donald Trump does not drink alcohol or smoke. His daughter Ivanka has converted to Judaism, which made him very proud and honored.

While the share of white Protestants and Catholics in the general electorate has slipped in recent presidential elections, the share of white evangelicals has stayed relatively the same and remains a powerful voting block, composing 23% of the electorate in 2012 and 2008.

Trump's relationship with evangelical leaders goes back far longer than he has been running for president. According to previously reported tax documents, the Donald J. Trump

Foundation has given to numerous Christian causes in recent years, including $100,000 to the Billy Graham Evangelist Association in 2012, as well as other ministries as far away as Debra George Ministries in Texas and the Ramp Church in Lynchburg, Virginia.

He has said his favorite book is the Bible but declined to cite his favorite verse. Trump has had a bumpy run talking about religion. In July, he drew criticism for saying he has not asked God for forgiveness.

"If I do something wrong I just try to make it right," he said. "When we go in church and when I drink my little wine, which is about the only wine I drink, and have my little cracker, I guess that's a form of asking for forgiveness."

In recent weeks, he has tried to make up for the missteps. In Iowa last weekend at the Faith and Freedom Coalition dinner, he waved his childhood Bible given to him by his mother.

"I'm Christian, I'm a Presbyterian, can you believe?" he said.

Trump is increasingly courting a wing of the Republican Party that might seem resistant to him: the evangelical Christians.

Trump had kind words for Pope Francis as the Catholic leader but mentioned that he disagrees with Francis on global warming. "He is a unifier. He wants to bring people together, and I think that's a great thing," Trump said. "That's what we have to do. We have to bring people together."

Trump hosts a group of evangelical pastors and bishops at Trump Tower in New York. Several attendees, including Pastor Lionel Traylor of Jackson, Mississippi, said that evangelical voters are particularly drawn to Trump's direct style and to his strong defense of Christians at a time "when Christianity is under attack.

Trump has frequently referred to attacks on Christians abroad and said that he will be a champion for religious liberty, including defending Christmas.

"I found him to be a humble man," said Dr. Darrell Scott, the senior pastor of New Spirit Revival Ministries in Cleveland Heights, Ohio, who met Trump at a similar gathering of pastors about four years ago.

"Many Christians know him personally and have had private conversations with him over the years," Cohen said, "And despite the fact that some of their views might be different, they certainly respect the fact that he speaks openly, he speaks from his heart, and he's willing to listen."

POLITICS

Donald Trump contributed to campaigns of both Republican Party and Democratic Party candidates over two decades of U.S. elections. Trump was an early supporter of Ronald Reagan for President of the United States. The Wall Street Journal poll released in March 2011 found that Trump was leading among potential contenders for the Republican Nomination, ahead of Mitt Romney. A Newsweek poll conducted in February 2011 showed Trump within a few points of President Barack Obama, with many undecided voters. The poll released in April of 2011 by Public Policy Polling showed Trump having a nine-point lead in a potential contest for the Republican Nomination while he was still considering a run.

Trump then announced he would not run for president.

In December 2011, Donald Trump was named among the top six of the ten most admired men and women living, according to a Gallop poll.

At the 2011 CPAC conference, Trump stated at a Tea Party supporters that he is pro-life and against gun control.

In February 2012, Trump endorsed Mitt Romney for President of the United States. He has called for stronger negotiations with China on trade and tariffs if necessary. Trump has advocated a policy and stronger leadership to deal with OPEC, which he has blamed for high oil prices.

In 2013, Trump was a featured speaker at the CPAC, and spent over $1 million to research a possible run for president. In October 2013, New York Republicans had circulated a memo suggesting Trump should run for Governor of the State of New York in 2014 against Andrew Cuomo. Trump said that while New York had problems and taxes are too high, running for Governor is not of great interest to him.

In January 2013, Trump endorsed Israeli Prime Minister Benjamin Netanyahu during the 2013 Israeli elections, stating that a strong prime minister is a strong Israel. In 2015, Trump was awarded the 'Liberty Award' at the 'Algemeiner Jewish 100 Gala' in honor of his positive contributions to US-Israel Relations.

UNIVISION

During his presidential campaign kickoff speech, Trump had portrayed immigrants from Mexico as "bringing drugs, they're bringing crime, they're rapists, and some, I assume, are good people." He also called for building a wall along the southern border of the U.S. The remarks drew condemnation from the Mexican government as "biased and absurd," and sparked Univision's announcement.

Trump has declared that his criticism was directed against U.S. policymakers, not the Mexican people or its government, and that Univision would be defaulting on an ironclad contract if it does not air the pageants. He pledged to take legal action against the Univision Company.

"They don't want me saying that Mexico is killing the United States in trade and killing the United States at the border," Trump had said.

Univision called Donald Trump's Mexican immigrant remarks as "insulting." Firing back at Univision for its refusal to air his Miss USA and Miss Universe Pageants, the outspoken mogul and GOP presidential candidate has barred anyone who works for Univision from the greens of his Miami golf course.

A letter from Donald Trump was dispatched a day after Univision declared it was canceling its coverage of the Miss USA pageant. Donald Trump told Univision: Get off my lawn.

In a letter to Randy Falco, Trump advised the Univision CEO that "under no circumstances is any officer or representative of Univision allowed to use Trump National Doral, Miami — its golf courses or any of its facilities."

Trump demanded that Falco and Univision's Miami Office location next door to Trump National Doral "immediately stop his work and close the gate which is being constructed between our respective properties."

Trump gave Falco one week to take care of that matter, or "we will close it."

"They can't back out." Trump added, "Pressure was put on

them by the Mexican government, in my opinion. Because I'm running for President, and as you know I'm polling very well, second place, but I'm running for President and I bring up the trade with Mexico is a disaster and the borders are a disaster. They want me to be quiet and not talk about that because Mexico wants to continue to rip off the United States and I won't allow that. That's all this is. It's disgraceful that Univision is on the same side as Mexico, and not on the side of the United States."

"They can do whatever they want." Trump said, "I couldn't care less. All I'm doing is fighting for the United States. I'm not fighting for Mexico."

THE RISE OF DONALD TRUMP

Trump is the very definition of the American success story, continually setting the standards of excellence while expanding his interests in real estate, sports and entertainment. He is a graduate of the Wharton School of Finance. Trump has authored over fifteen bestsellers, and his first book, The Art of the Deal, is considered a business classic and one of the most successful business books of all time.

But for the GOP presidential candidates, Donald Trump's candidacy presented a debacle. Some of them were outspoken against Trump. Rick Perry called him a "cancer on conservatism." Ron Paul even expressed his dislike for Trump, forecasting that he would "rule with an iron fist" if elected. Nonetheless, latest polls show Trump leading all other Republicans.

Most people view politics like they view a religion. They enjoy politicians who resemble their religious leaders such as a preacher and against anyone who is not for them. They are attracted to a candidate who claims to have the answers to everything, and promise to take immediate action when given that power. In short, the people want a King.

This dogmatic approach to politics becomes a highly divided political climate. Trump is perceived as anti-establishment and many like him for that and among other qualities he has.

"We are going to make our country great again," with a commitment to become the "greatest jobs president that God ever created."

(Remember the movie "The Good the Bad and the Ugly?
Tuco is in a bubble bath. A Man enters the room.
Man: I've been looking for you for 8 months. Whenever I should have had a gun in my right hand, I thought of you. Now I find you in exactly the position that suits me. I had lots of time to learn to shoot with my left.
With the gun he has hidden in the foam, Tuco kills him.
Tuco: When you have to shoot, shoot. Don't talk."

TRUMP'S CAMPAIGN

Trump has campaigned extensively in Iowa, New Hampshire, Las Vegas and Los Angeles.

On July 11, 2015, more than 9,000 people registered to attend Trump's rally at the Phoenix Convention Center. At over-capacity, the crowd of thousands watched Trump speak for more than an hour. His remarks were centered on illegal immigration, the event was hosted by the Republican Party, and Trump was introduced by Sheriff Joe Arpaio. Trump invoked Richard Nixon's "silent majority" speech, saying, "The silent majority is back."

Investigative journalist Sharyl Attkisson detailed how the Washington Post took Trump's remarks on McCain out of context. She stated, "In fact, Trump's actual quote is the opposite of what is presented in the Post's first sentence."

On July 21, Trump publicly gave out Senator Lindsey Graham's phone number during a speech in South Carolina, as a response to Graham, calling him a "jackass". Graham released a statement on Twitter that he would "probably [be] getting a new phone" and later released a video in which he destroyed his phone.

On August 21, Trump held a campaign rally at the Ladd-Peebles Stadium in Mobile, Alabama, with approximately 30,000 people in attendance.

Donald Trump has hired serious strategists as he gets going on his presidential bid. Corey Lewandowski is the campaign manager for Donald Trump's 2016 presidential campaign. She is a New Hampshire-based veteran of the Koch brothers, Americans for Prosperity. The former South Carolina House Majority Leader James Merrill is an adviser. Chuck Laudner, who helped Rick Santorum win the 2012 Iowa GOP caucus, is running his Hawkeye State efforts.

Former Federal Elections Commission Chairman Don McGahn is on board and helped Trump set up the legal framework of his campaign.

"He's actually hired some serious staffers," said GOP strategist Ford O'Connell.

Trump says he will self-fund his campaign.

"You're going to be well taken care of working for him. As

an operative that's an attractive thing," said O'Connell.

Lewandowski said that Trump "has the largest staff," and insisted, "There is no premium paid by Mr. Trump because of his vast wealth. My salary is very commensurate with what Mitt Romney paid his campaign manager four years ago."

Trump's campaign headquarters is on the fifth floor of Trump Tower, in an industrial space that previously was a construction area and hangout for the crew of NBC's "The Apprentice." The main room is a showcase for Trump's penchant for boastful teasing: A "wall of shame" features downcast photos of the two candidates who have dropped out, Scott Walker and Governor Rick Perry. It also highlights his ability to create a sting operation as his aides work on plastic picnic tables and sit on folding chairs.

With hundreds of staffers on the payroll Trump's Manhattan command center can fit inside the expansive space of the Brooklyn headquarters of Hillary Clinton, without being noticed. Lewandowski said about a dozen aides are at the location, including political director Michael Glassner and Representative Hope Hicks.

Trump has between seven and 12 paid staffers in each of the first three voting states - Iowa, New Hampshire and South Carolina, and is hiring in Florida, Georgia, Tennessee, Texas and other states. Lewandowski said Trump enjoys a "massive grass-roots network," allowing volunteers to feed local intelligence on the rival campaigns.

His advisers are working to assure that Trump will qualify for the ballot in all 50 states and the U.S. territories, a time-consuming task that has caused some first-time candidates to stumble. The Trump campaign has hired a company that will work only for meeting the state-by-state requirements.

Trump presented a combative persona than the one that is familiar to the public on television. He was at ease, thoughtful at times, but still displaying high sensitivity to any unfair media coverage. Trump has often said he is a counterpuncher who attacks primarily when provoked.

"I'm a person who is capable of going into far greater detail than any of my opponents," he said, "I've never had a voter stand up and say, 'Could you release policy papers?',"

Trump picked up a campaign bumper sticker featuring his name in thick red letters and declared smiling proudly. "A hot ticket,"

"I believe in the power of positive thinking," Trump said, "but I never like to talk about it. It's never in sight until you win it. You know, there are a lot of minefields out there."

Trump said he disagreed with predictions that the contest will narrow to two or three finalists for the nomination.

"In the end you'll have at least four or five candidates." He said, signifying that the RNC will try and control the election outcome till the end.

Since announcing his presidential campaign, Trump has been saying things the Media did not want you to know. For example, he has been talking about the dangers posed by illegal immigration; criminals and rapists pouring over the open border.

FINANCING

In April 2011, Trump weighed in running as a candidate in the US Presidential Election of 2012. Politico quoted that if Trump should decide to run for President, he would file "financial disclosure statements that show his net worth in excess of $7 billion with more than $250 million of cash, and very little debt."

Although Trump did not run as a candidate in the 2012 elections, his professionally prepared 2012 financial disclosure was published in his book stating a $7 billion net worth.

In 2015, Forbes estimated his net worth at $4.1 billion. Business Insider has his net worth estimated at 8.7 billion based on public audits. Trump himself said he is worth over $10 Billion.

On June 16, 2015, prior to announcing his candidacy for President, Trump released professionally prepared financial disclosure statements to the media stating a net worth of over $9 billion.

Trump, who is mostly self-funding his campaign, said he had originally budgeted up to $20 million through mid-September for television advertising. But so far, he did not spend any money to be on the airwaves. "It's been all Trump, all the time."

He and his aides said that would soon change. His campaign has hired a Florida-based advertising firm, and Trump said he has proposed several concepts for ads in the works.

"I have such a great concept." Trump said, declining to specify.

Campaign manager Corey Lewandowski said Trump's team would probably spend considerably more than $20 million on paid media later this year — "whatever it takes." He said the spots would be "nontraditional," saying the firm that he and Trump declined to name, has never created political ads.

Central to the fall strategy is the release later this month of a book that will serve as a campaign manifesto.

Trump does not believe the next stage of the campaign will require him to change his flamboyant, confrontational style, which has captivated the attention of voters whether they support him or not. But he noted that running for president has brought pressures and demands that he did not experience in the business world and had not anticipated in the political arena.

Donald Trump vowed to win the Presidency saying, "I'm not going anywhere."

Trump said he does not want to tinker with how he presents himself to the public. Trump wants to remain Trump.

"You've got to have a personality." Trump said. "You've got to be able to speak your mind. You've got to have some thoughts that are correct."

In the third quarter of campaign financing, the "self-funded" Trump contributed a mere $100,800 to his own campaign and spent more than $500,000 on hats from Louisiana-based Ace Specialties. Together with T-shirts, his campaign spent $678,000 on apparel, more than it spent on any other line item except for airfare and since all airfare was paid to a Trump-owned airline, "Make America Great Again" merchandise was effectively the candidates largest outside expense.

Trump financed his wholesale hat purchases by taking in $3.8 million in outside contributions, more than many other GOP candidates who never claimed to be self-funding. That

$3.8 million was made up of 74,000 individual donations, a portion of which came in the form of merchandise purchases. Trump can't directly profit off sales of campaign merchandise, but those sales do make it easier for him to sustain a campaign without spending very much of his own money.

In the previous quarter, Trump contributed $1.8 million to his own cause while taking in just $96,300 in outside contributions. The candidate credited his drastic reduction in self-financing to "good business practices," among other things, in a statement:

While our original budget was substantially higher than the amount spent, good business practices and even better ideas and policy have made it unnecessary to spend a larger sum.

Still, Trump is raising just barely enough to sustain his current spending. His campaign took in $5.8 million since it launched, and spent it all except for the $254,000.

Trump recently told the Washington Post that he's on the verge of making his first big ad buy. To do so, Trump needs to increase his personal spending. In the alternative, he could just continue riding a steady stream of free media and ever-increasing trucker-hat word-of-mouth marketing to the Republican Nomination — the latest CBS News poll puts him atop the primary field with 27 percent of the vote.

POLLS

Donald Trump is pulling ahead in polls across key states, building a lead that seems to squash the storyline.

CNN, NBC, and FOX polls show every week Trump's growing support in all states with double-digit leads.

There is no other candidate with double-digit support in any state.

Donald Trump is building his lead in the polls. He has drawn about 25 to 35 percent, to show that voter support is growing for his brand of politics. The numbers from the recent polls show even more good signs for Donald Trump.

The economy, 67% of Republicans in all polled states said Trump.

Foreign policy, 34% said Trump.

Illegal immigration, a whopping 55% said Trump.

ISIS, the militant group, 46% said Trump.

Trump has become the major point of attack for those trailing him in the polls, namely Jeb Bush. The former Florida Governor released a two-minute video mocking Trump and calling him unfit to lead America's military.

Donald Trump has frequently traded barbs with Jeb Bush. This week Trump also took aim at Jeb's brother, former President George W. Bush. Trump said Bush was at least partly to blame for 9/11 for failing to stop the attacks.

The voters seem to be more interested when he is critical and less politically correct. Trump has now led the race for several months, and his lead is continuing to grow.

Trump himself has touted the poll numbers, sharing them with fans through his Instagram page showing him nearly doubling up Ben Carson. Jeb Bush and Marco Rubio last year were considered as frontrunners. Neither Jeb Bush nor Marco Rubio are able to crack double digits, and now suffer behind Trump at third and fifth place.

The latest poll released, revealed that 500 Republican Primary voters consider Trump as their favorite top choice.

Trump has momentum on his side as he continues to gain support from Republican voters in early primary states like

New Hampshire, Iowa, and South Carolina as voters emphasize the increasingly strong desire for a Republican candidate with a proven business record and not a traditional politician.

POLITICAL MEDIA

The hovering reporters move with Trump like a swarm of bees. Every time he closes his mouth, they shout questions.

Trump is such a popular candidate that they are attacking him just to get themselves noticed.

The media are full of others explanations of Trump, criticisms of Trump, justifications of Trump, analyses of Trump, and any outrageous thing Trump has done. He is on the front page of every newspaper, the top of every newscast. They can't believe that this is happening, and not only is it happening, it is the biggest thing in American politics right now. It has consumed American politics. Trump is bigger than the entire Republican field, NBC and CNN putt together, to include the 15 other Governors, and

Senators. Trump is bigger than they are.

Trump is unpredictable. And that's how he likes it to stay. He's the only unpredictable Presidential candidate in recent memory. This is a major plus because the press cannot target him, directly or indirectly. They'll attack him on point A, and he responds with his own attack, or replies with a non sequitur, or he just changes the subject because he is bored with the reporters.

He says something culturally and politically incorrect, and the press jackals go after him with flashing teeth and claws, fully expecting to take him down, demanding him to beg, but he shrugs his shoulders, and his approval ratings go up.

Above all, he is mentioning taboo subjects.

Putting the press into the wall is worth celebrating. Reporters want Trump to be something they can identify, and then they want to assault that... but he keeps shifting grounds, and putting on new moves and faces. He drives them crazy.

In addition, the crowds at his speeches are building up. One of these days, he'll easily fill a football stadium.

The press hates that. If Trump ever resorts to elaborate on issues, the press will bring on an army of experts to refute him "on the facts."

When it comes to election campaigns, you have to understand that the job of the media is to grind down every candidate to a small series of meaningless clichés.

The press wants empty generalities. They want androids for candidates in the debates. They want to make a possible something into nothing. This political correctness goes largely unnoticed.

Trump has broken the mold and the media says he must pay. The media is out for revenge but something has gone wrong. Not as far as Trump was concerned, and not as far as the public was concerned.

Trump has triggered a response from a public that feels they have been in strait jackets for too long. They cannot say this, they cannot say that and they cannot look to Presidents for solutions. Presidents should spout rhetorical bullshit.

So, a man shows up who seems to feel the same way they do and isn't afraid to say so.

The press doesn't know what to do. Every line they feed Trump, in an effort to slam him, becomes the occasion for one of his biggest comebacks and is carried to the next day.

Although Trump seems to improvise and play their game faster than they, he actually plays his own game and does it right out in the open. The same media who made Trump famous worldwide for decades are now looking at him with great disbelief. They cannot cast him off like an old dog, he is now front and center.

For decades, the press controlled the Presidential Campaign events by favoring those candidates who adopt their lies and promote them in front of television viewers. By running the Campaign debates the media influences the viewers of their own choice of candidate to win in every election.

But right now, Trump has showed up.

Making a joke of him does not help, either. People laugh at the joke not at Trump.

You can be sure that the major networks are trying to figure out how to torpedo Trump. This is supposed to be **their** Presidential Campaign, not his. They own the franchise. But he's ripping huge chunks out of their fleeces. That was not supposed to happen, but more and more people are noticing it. Every time Trump hits a home run against one of these smug bloodless low life media people, it is an occasion for great delight.

Trump is doing much more than gaining ground on the other candidates; he is attacking the whole framework of this narrated Show.

An interview with Trump isn't an interview. The only thing the networks can do is try to shut him out. Republicrats are media puppets, and not better than him. On the media front, he is visibly dominant. Trump is too big to fail and networks set themselves up in planning new battles to the public. But Trump punched a hole in their own illusion of winning and he is an imminent threat to them.

Trump is so big they are attacking him just to get themselves noticed. Lindsey Graham, the senator from South Carolina, called Trump a "jackass," so Trump gave out his cell-phone number on national television, and suddenly Lindsey Graham, languishing at less than one percent in the polls, was all anybody was talking about. You're welcome, Lindsey Graham.

Donald Trump opposed granting any rights or concessions for illegal aliens. Throughout the period of his campaign, he absorbs attacks on both sides of the political spectrum, both on social networks and news channels.

Trump tells why people do not trust the media. And here is why. He establishes that 60% to 70% of the political media is dishonest. Some of them are great. For example, he talks about the American dream in his speeches. Trump said "The American dream is dead but I'm going to make it bigger, better and stronger than ever before." Later on he reads in the newspapers, 'The American dream is dead'.

Donald Trump blasted the media in another bombastic interview, saying that some journalists are "among the worst people he's ever met."

"I don't like lies, I don't mind a bad story," Trump told "60

Minutes." "If you did a bad story on me for 60 Minutes, if it were a fair story I wouldn't be thin-skinned at all."

"They write lies, they write false stories. They know they are false. It makes no difference."

"I could take it if it's fair," Trump said. "If people say things that are false which happens a lot with me, if people say things that are false I will fight like harder than anybody."

"If I do something wrong, and that happens, and they write a fair story that I did something wrong, there's nothing to fight about. I can handle that. I do not like lying. You know I'm a very honorable guy, I don't like lies,"

CHANCE OF WINNING

Trump started flirting with the idea of running for President since 1988. In 2011, he also led in the polls for several months, but eclipsed over time and then withdrew. In the era where people can vent their anger in social networking and intensify it a thousand times, Trump was always considered a charismatic performer and a privileged tycoon. This year Trump enjoyed another advantage - he could tap his followers and win applause from the audience on whatever subject he decides to talk about.

Trump's coverage in the news has skyrocketed making him one of the most talked about man in America. That could ultimately help him should he flame out of the race, considering how important name recognition is to his bottom line.

Before Trump seriously considered running, he looked at the chance of other candidates to be elected. Trump was not surprised to find that many voters channel their frustration to find an outsider to resolve their problems.

From the end of President Reagan's term in office through the Obama Administration, U.S. Government policies have shown a record loss in jobs and financial hardship. This in turn has destroyed the stabilizing force of the middle class. It has become harder and harder to make a living. The voters want someone who will renew them, excite them, someone to speak from the gut, without fear in opposing the two parties, unlike John McCain and Mitt Romney - who lost the election to Barack Obama. The voters are looking for the candidate who does not depend on billionaire donors that dominate over both parties. A candidate who isn't afraid to criticize either gender with remarks and kick out politically correct media ideology without being discouraged. And Trump delivers the goods. He manages to throw his opponents out of the ring.

SUPER PAC

Political Action Committee (PAC) is a popular term for a purpose of raising and spending money to elect and defeat candidates. Most PACs represent business, labor or ideological interests. They can give up to $15,000 annually to any national party committee, and $5,000 annually to any other PAC. PACs may receive up to $5,000 from any individual. Many politicians also form Leadership PACs as a way of raising money to help fund other candidates' campaigns.

Super PACs are a relatively new type of committee and may raise unlimited sums of money from corporations, unions, associations and individuals, then spend unlimited sums for or against political candidates.

Unlike traditional PACs, super PACs are prohibited from donating money directly to political candidates. Super PACs are required to report their donors to the Federal Election Commission on a monthly basis in off years, and in the year of an election.

As of October 16, 2015, there were more than 1100 groups, which were organized as super PACs. They have reported total proceeds of $300 million.

Trump has complained repeatedly that Super PACs allow corporate entities and lobbyists to have undue influence. He said that because he is self-funding the bulk of his campaign he is not obligated to any special interests.

"I have disavowed all Super PACs, requested the return of all donations made to said PACs, and I am calling on all presidential candidates to do the same,"

Carl Icahn said he would create new groups to fight corporate "inversions" and change the tax code.

THE KOCH BROTHERS

The Koch brothers become the nation's third wealthiest individuals. Placing Charles and David Koch's net worth at $51.7 billion each. They have donated more than $100 million to dozens of free-market and advocacy organizations. They also contribute to 34 political and policy organizations three of which they founded, and several of which they direct, all to influence the political system, and accumulate more wealth and power. It was clear to the RNC that the Koch brothers will solidify their takeover of the Republican Party.

The Koch's political operation aims to influence the Republican Party's master voter files, gaining influence over the GOP.

The Koch brothers are trying to take over the party, and the party has been more than happy to take their millions from them. Politicians are happy to sell their souls to the Koch's if that means they win.

After shunning the GOP for decades, Charles and David Koch try to take it over. The Koch's deep-pocket political organizations plan to spend $889 million by the end of 2016 to drive its free-market policy and Philanthropic Agenda as well as, direct the electorate support to the candidate of their choosing.

They want to take over the whole party, which means controlling the White House, Congress, and the keys to all the data of all the Republican voters. That is what happens when you lie in the mud with pigs.

But then the Donald came to town...

The Republican Party's ongoing civil war involves a lot of fireworks and sub-plots; but the overreaching fight remains between two visions and the three billionaires.

Charles and David Koch are investing hundreds of millions of dollars for the GOP control, and aim to push America towards libertarianism. Donald Trump joined the Republican Party to run for President and push the country in the opposite direction, toward nationalism.

Unfortunately, the Koch's made several mistakes, and are steadily handing victories to the Donald.

Many voters might be surprised to learn these men are so different. After all, they bear some similarities. They treat each other politely; David and Donald, for instance, have socialized together in Florida.

The Koch brothers' critique of Washington is almost the exact opposite of Trump's opinion. From the 1960s through the George W. Bush Administration, Charles and David Koch were fierce critics of the GOP. David Koch, in fact, was the Libertarian Party candidate for Vice President in 1980, the same year Ronald Reagan was first elected. The two brothers founded and funded think tanks to oppose the Vietnam War, the Patriot Act, homophobic marriage laws, corporate subsidies, deficit spending, and many other GOP positions.

The policies where they actually agree with Trump are climate change and health reform. Charles and David feared that Obama socialized medicine, and his overreaction on climate change, will crash the economy. As a result, they discarded their careful libertarian strategy and created a new party. They heavily backed the GOP by funding the Tea Party movement, built to attack Obama and the Democrats.

But in the short period, the Koch investment clearly failed. The Tea Party failed to block Obama's election victories; failed to block healthcare reform; failed to block healthcare implementation; and failed to block executive action on climate change. By attacking the Democratic Party directly, the Koch brothers dragged their own brand into the political arena, which was exactly what they wanted to avoid.

The Tea Party may have been a bad platform for the Koch brothers' vision, but it is almost perfect for Trump, who leads both the GOP race and the Tea Party. Meanwhile, Trump is picking up the pieces.

The Tea Party has made a turn towards Trump. When the Koch brothers tried to block Trump from access to their political network in July; Trump turned it to his advantage and by August, many key operatives were abandoning the Koch network in favor of Trump. On this course, the Koch brothers' billion-dollar bet on the GOP is not to elect their worst enemy as President.

The Koch network is giving Cruz, Walker, Rubio, Bush and Paul a platform to share their ideas at well-lighted, well-attended events in early primary states like New Hampshire, Iowa and Nevada.

But Scott Walker, the Koch brothers' favorite, has dropped out. Rand Paul, The sole libertarian in the race is losing fast and barely exists.

The Koch brothers still have a play. With an estimated $100 billion in combined personal net worth, they have more than 10 times the resources available to Trump. They still hope that American voters will step up and shut down the Donald. They may try to promote one of Trump's competitors, such as Marco Rubio or John Kasich, or even Carly Fiorina and Jeb Bush could be good candidates for the Koch brothers. It is hard to see how the Koch brothers ultimately get what they want by continuing to fund the GOP. It is time for them to cut their losses.

The Koch brothers gathered 450 top conservative donors at a lush oceanfront hotel but Donald Trump was not invited to their powerful political network.

Therefore, Trump turned the Twitter on and mocked Gov. Jeb Bush, Marco Rubio, Scott Walker, Ted Cruz and Carly Fiorina - who were given an entrée at the luxurious gathering.

"I wish good luck to all the Republican candidates who traveled to California to beg for money from the Koch Brothers," Trump tweeted Sunday. "Puppets?"

Trump's provocative jab charged the Koch brothers with an

attempt to buy influence, but at the same time, he attacked the integrity of the five candidates, asking for a fight. The Donald does what the Donald does, and he does not need anyone's money to fund his Presidential Campaign,

However, the Koch brothers have indicated that they are unlikely to settle on one Republican candidate when they are looking at a strong field of candidates aligned with their policy goals. The truth is that the Koch brothers are afraid that Donald Trump will be elected after all, and they will lose everything without any hope for recovery.

The Democrats have spent tens of millions of dollars seeking to vilify the Koch's and their agenda, portraying them as wealthy industrialists who have put the disadvantaged at risk to help their candidates who came there for donation without showing any hesitation in seeking their favor.

For the most part, Donald Trump ignores them all.

Walker, who was aided by Koch, said before quitting the race that he wished "the whole world could see what goes on here" at the Koch network gatherings.

Bush, who received a very warm reception from Koch network donors, said he was honored to take part in the forum.

DEBATES

Under the Fox News rules, only the top 10 candidates with the highest national polling average will be included in the first debate.

Asked whether Trump will keep up the attacks, campaign manager Corey Lewandowski said he would. "They should be worried about Donald Trump."

There is a real concern, particularly on the debate stage, that Trump won't play by the rules and he's going to throw some below-the-belt punches. Republicans in a primary don't like to see the candidates attacking each other.

The challenge with somebody like Trump is that there is a sort of assumption that you're racing with professionals. It is a challenge because he's very unpredictable. Above all the Republican National Committee is nervous about Trump's rhetoric.

Several Iowa Republicans expressed dismay at Trump's momentum, labeling him as someone whose brash personality and celebrity status make him a bad fit for the rural first nominating state.

Party insiders acknowledge what most of the Republicans think, 'What have we done to let a guy like Donald Trump on the debate stage?'

All those who are fed up altogether with the political system, are drawn to Trump.

Donald Trump stepped into a hornet's nest when it came to the debate. The ten rivals did not shy away from trying to sting him.

Trump swiftly returned fire, living up to his reputation as the bulldogs attack him.

"In Wisconsin I went to No.1, and you went down the tubes," Trump retorted, highlighting Walker's slumping poll numbers.

The presumptive Jeb Bush, who is supported by the Koch brothers, is under intense pressure to deliver a breakout performance, or risk a campaign meltdown.

Bush, the campaign's ultimate Republican establishment, has seen his political fortunes tumble in the last months since Trump entered the race.

Lately, Bush experienced the power of Trump eating his lunch in his home base, Florida. The fact is his backdoor donors are not able to save him from the quick sand he entered.

While it is unclear whether Carson poses an immediate threat to Trump's dominance, the rise of the doctor, who like Trump, has never held public office is more evidence of an anti-establishment wave washing over the nomination race.

NBC's got a poll...CNN got a poll..., everyone got a poll. And Trump is really coming up in popularity among the crowd. These are establishment Republicans, actually. These people run around and complain about abortion and social issues. These people are all excited about Trump. Trump has set this up pretty well in terms of his performance on debates.

Trump said, "I don't debate. I'm a guy that gets things done. I tell everybody what to do and they go and do it. I make decisions and we make things happen. I don't sit around and debate all day. That's all these guys do. That's all these guys do is debate. I'm not good at it. I don't debate. There isn't anybody else's opinion that matters than mine."

So he's set up expectations that maybe he's not going to do well in this kind of format because this kind of format requires deference to the others.

Because it's predictable and stale. The candidates on a stage get three minutes, and then 30 seconds to reply, and then if somebody attacks you, you get 15.5 seconds to defend or whatever. At some point, Trump is going to say how stupid he thinks this is and how unproductive he thinks this is and what a waste of time. He will not say that because he is there.

Then you have the moderators trying to intersect and interject and keep control of the thing and trying to make names for themselves, too, even though they deny that.

Whoever the moderators are, they are going to try to get good publicity for asking the right questions or policing the thing well, Trump would think that when these debates are all said and done, what happens then?

It's going to be like everything else he's doing in the campaign. A breath of fresh air and people are going to be applauding him. Except the establishment media, who are going to worry about what does this mean for politics because they control it.

On the other hand, Trump is not controllable. When he is the only one on stage, he owns it, and is very confident, and all the things that go with that. Trump is not an ordinary, predictable candidate. The moderators determine what to discuss, unless a candidate or two decides to reach out and take control of the whole thing.

Another thing Trump has to consider, as a lone wolf candidate, the last thing Trump wants is that he is just one of the gang, just one of many contenders. It is destined to be fireworks of some kind. It has to be.

PEOPLE COMMENTS

- "Shark Tank" investor Kevin O'Leary said that Donald Trump is upsetting the political process and it will be positive for him as an entrepreneur. "I think it's good for his brand," O'Leary told Huff Post. "I think he's being honest when he talks to people." O'Leary noted that he does find Donald Trump refreshing outside-the-beltway demeanor. But if Trump hopes to be a real leader, he needs to tell Americans which people he'll choose to support his vision for the country. O'Leary explained: He's going to have to show us the voters that he can bring together a cabinet of very, very strong people to run the government. He is the vision guy, but I want to know who's going to be the secretary of state, who's going to run finance, who's going to support business, who's going to do all the things government has to do? Can he build a bureaucracy that keeps his vision? If he can do that, he can be President of the United States.

- As Trump marched out of the hotel after a speech, a large group of people just wanted to shake his hand and trail him. One woman positioned herself outside his shiny black SUV as he climbed inside.

"Mr. Trump!" she yelled. "God bless you! You changed everything!" Trump wound down the window halfway, smiled and waved, as the vehicle took him away from there.

"He's a little rough on the edges. He's not a politician," she said. "That's his good side."

- An 80-year-old retired comptroller Laquita Doris Ballew, who said she has little in common with the New York billionaire but she believes he cannot be bought by special interests.

"I'm opposed to socialism, and he's the ultimate capitalist," she said.

- Jase Robertson had no idea that simply asking where to find the restroom in the Trump Hotel would immediately get him escorted out of the building. But that is exactly what happened, according to Robertson, the star of A&E's Duck Dynasty. In fact, the Trump hotel employee pointed to

Central Park and told Robertson he could find a bathroom there. Robertson said a couple of years ago, I was escorted out of the Trump hotel, when I asked a guy where the bathroom is, he looked at me, 'Right this way,' he said and grabbed my arm, took me outside and pointed at Central Park and said, 'Have a nice day.'

This incident resulted in a friendship with the Trump family, as trump called to apologize when he heard about the incident. Robertson particularly bonded with Trump's son, Donald Trump Jr. who invited Robertson to spend some time with Trump Jr., on and off the golf course.

"We actually really hit it off because he has a heart for kids with the same condition as Mia," Robertson said, referring to his daughter's cleft lip and palate. "I had no idea of that at the time, and when I learned that and saw what Willie did, I was like, 'Well, anyone who has a heart for kids with cleft lip and palate is a positive on my list."

In a recent interview, Robertson stated that he likes Donald Trump for President and that he's excited about the candidates the Republican Party has for President this year.

▪ "Funny how no one from the lame stream media (FOX included) God, but these media people are low down and slimy. As regards to Latinos and blacks, it seems they also believe their own BS."

- "Every time the media try to do something, negative to Trump it backfires. This publicity is just more positive for Trump. And it's free!"

- "That nice woman, all she did was buying a PEOPLE MAGAZINE and now she has CNN political attack dogs out on her? Well, she seems to me to be quite able, assertive, and enthusiastic in her own right and I have a feeling the media's in for a great big surprise. She is no Joe Plummer questioning a candidate's views, and they are going to find that out. This woman loves Donald Trump and loves America and that is all they're going to get out of her: LOVE FOR TRUMP!"

- "I love him," said Jeanne Sangenario. "Because I know he would take no baloney from anybody from any world leader and he would get things done and the economy would come back big time, he would get it done. No two ways about it."

- "He's the only person who tells the truth," Chatsworth resident Miriam Williamson emphatically said.

- Curtis Whitlock echoed those sentiments and added, "He says what he thinks instead of what he thinks is politically correct."

- Marietta resident Ben Hendricks said he liked Trump's commitment to military strength. He asserted that people feel the nation isn't flexing its position as a world leader as much as they would like. Hendricks said he feels Trump would reverse that.

"He's not scared," he said.

"You could take the five major news networks and filter Jesus Christ, Buddha, Hitler, Stalin, Attila, Gandhi, and Lawrence Welk. Candidate after candidate lies through his teeth, and the people buy in."

- "I for one will not vote for Bush. I live in Florida and he is a real jerk. He is one of the elite, and does not have time for peons. He is probably mad that his brother has been President and now he wants it at all costs. I will vote against all Republican officeholders if they force Bush on us. If the Republicans want to nominate another moderate, I am all out."

- "Bush III is running scared, if he takes a scorching in this race from Trump, his political career is over and done, stick a fork in it. With Benson and Trump commanding over 50% of the vote there is zero chance for any of the career politicians to do anything, anything at all to get in contention."

TRUMP RALLIES

America is in a decline, losing jobs and industry to China and Mexico, and losing oil to the Middle East. Barack Obama is stupid. The other presidential candidates are also stupid, or boring. Wealthy donors, who pay for their campaigns control them all, and are dark forces pulling the strings backstage. Money is the real puppet-master in America. Trump knows this because he's rolling in it, and he's been controlling politicians all his life.

Now only Donald Trump, a smart, successful, property tycoon and TV celebrity so rich he is beholden to no one, can fix the problem. He will bring jobs, take care of veterans and the elderly, and be the most militaristic person in the room.

The audience loves every second of it, especially those parts that parody the political establishment, such as when Trump does an impression of a stiff politician.

"Ladies and gentlemen," he says, as monotone politician. His shoulders are hunched, his eyes squinting at an imaginary script near the podium. "Hello," he says. There are howls of laughter.

"You don't want a scripted President!" he tells them, as people rise to their feet for a standing ovation and the loudest applause of the night. As the crescendo builds, he adds "And you don't want a politically correct President!"

Now he's in the Oval Office, taking a call from the chief executive of Ford, who wants to build a factory in Mexico. President Trump tells him he will not permit that to happen. The auto manufacturer protests, so Trump tells him he'll slap a 35% tax on every Ford car and truck brought to America. The CEO gives in and the crowd cheers wildly. "It's that simple," Trump, tells them. "Believe me."

Toward the end of his speech, Trump stops, mid-sentence, apparently lost in thought. He points to the back of the auditorium.

"Look at all the cameras blazing there," he says. "This is live, all over the place. We're on Fox, CNN."

He picks up an invisible script from the podium. "Look," he

adds, "there's nothing."

People line up to hear Donald Trump speak at a campaign rallies.

Outside every rally, there is always another crowd. These people could not get into the main event or the overflow room. They have been waiting outside for hours and now Trump's private security guards, who are playing the part of secret service agents, are holding them back.

Someone throws a bunch of flowers that hit Trump in the face. He smiles, waves, and gets into a presidential-style motorcade of SUVs with blacked-out windows.

"Thank you Trump," shrieks a woman as the car door slams shut. "For giving us hope."

It is nearly impossible not to be at or near the top of the polls when you get that much attention.

More than seven hours before doors opened, ticket holders began lining up outside, hoping to get a good seat for the rally.

Wearing a blue suit with a red striped tie Trump paused for photos and autographs before taking the podium. He is critical of news coverage of his campaign.

THE SILENT MAJORITY

It is a known fact that all of this country's money belongs to 1% of the population. It is also known that 80% of all new income goes to that 1%. The middle class is observably shrinking. There is a silent majority in favor of Trump. Both sides represent extremes whoever wins will set the precedent for what the future of politics will look like.

Richard Nixon made the phrase "silent majority" popular. Trump has noticed early in his campaign, that the "silent majority" is back in business in America. He said the crowds of people—hundreds of thousands, millions of the silent majority nationwide are getting involved in the election process and are not silent anymore.

"They want to see America become great again." Trump said.

"They are waking up and fighting to take back the country from the political class."

Trump predicted that he will not only win the White House in 2016, but that he will be re-elected in 2020 and that at the end of his eventual eight years in the White House he will be known to all as a "great conservative" just like Ronald Reagan.

A Hispanic woman named Myriam Witcher went on stage at the Republican Presidential Candidate Donald Trump's Las Vegas rally, and acknowledged her love for Trump.

When asked if she had ever met Trump before being on stage with him, Witcher said, "Only in my dreams. You are not going to believe what I am going to tell you. I believe in law attraction. I believe in being a positive person. And three nights before he came to Las Vegas, I told my husband, 'Oh, I have dreams. You can't imagine. I saw Mr. Trump in my dreams. And I saw him like I had the opportunity to give him a hug.' And I had my Facebook page, and I wrote so many times, Mr. Trump, I am a Hispanic person, and I hope I have the opportunity to give a hug to you. He doesn't know me. In my pictures — I don't have pictures in Facebook about myself."

When she was asked if Trump's comments about mass deportations and Mexican rapists bothered her Witcher said, "It doesn't bother me at all. Mr. Trump is 100 percent right," she added, "He is my perfect man, everything he says is absolutely right."

However, think about how the media and especially CNN track down Trump's supporter, taking her to a media outlet for a live-feed and then beginning their inquisition of her. Why is it that CNN stops here and does not extend the same level of energy tracking other talking heads?

Donald Trump represents freedom, pride, masculinity, and he is saying no to political correctness. The silent majority are listening.

BARACK OBAMA

Obama was an unknown, obscure former state legislator who had not completed a single term as U.S. senator, but he was canny. He came from nowhere and won it all - twice. All the previously prevailing standards, all the usual expectations, were thrown out the window. Every talking head in Washington, DC said it is up to Americans to decide whether a candidate is worthy of power.

The fact remains, that voters have seen all kinds of experienced or ill-prepared candidates over the years.

Trump's rise is not the result of President Obama crippling America for eight years. It is the result of the Republican base embracing a strong candidate.

Trump has frequently used his platform to educate the public on the failures of this administration. Trump believes in the Free Market, a strong military and our country's sacred obligation to take care of our veterans and their families.

Trump clearly sickened over Obama Presidency, whom he also regards him as weak and unworthy. Trump questioning whether Obama had good enough grades to enter to Harvard Law School and his proof of citizenship. Trump called for Obama to end the citizenship issue by releasing the long-form of his birth certificate. He said Obama lacked the winner qualities and has had so many losses that the Country's reputation is debilitated.

"The president is not psychologically tough. If he had it, Vladimir Putin would not be eating his lunch. He does not have it and he never will. It's not in his DNA."

On the other side, Obama made a formal statement and released the short-form of his birth certificate.

Trump prospered like no one else in converting his celebrity status into a successful candidate.

HILLARY CLINTON

Trump, argued Clinton is facing an FBI investigation on the emails, and they just let her off. He was surprised to see other potential candidates, who should not have been in the race.

In the Trump world, the two parties don't just have different political philosophies. They represent two different universes.

Donald Trump claims that Bernie Sanders let Hillary Clinton "off the hook" and that he is a socialist/communist and a Maniac.

Donald Trump noticed that Hillary Clinton is becoming loud and obnoxious. He dinged Hillary Clinton for using a teleprompter during her campaign speeches: "What kind of speech is that? That's not a speech," he declared.

Donald Trump says Hillary Clinton will likely win the Democratic nomination because she is being "protected" from any consequences stemming from her use of a private email server.

Hillary and Donald have one thing in common; they can both negotiate a deal.

In the case of The Donald, he is seeking deals that increase his own brand: real estate, development rights, partnerships, investments and even media contracts. He gambles his own assets, his own reputation, and his own advantage. And he wins or loses his own money.

In the case of Hillary Clinton, she increased the value of the Clinton Foundation, negotiated deals to benefit herself and Bill, or the Foundation by using assets of the US government to her advantage, and our country's reputation. Had she not been Bill's wife, Obama's Secretary of State, how much advantage would she yield? What would she have to hold up her side?

It is high time that our government representatives cease and desist from using the assets that do not belong to them to feather their own nest.

When asked about the Democrat's potential run for the White House, Gov. Mike Huckabee described her as 'smart' and 'tough,' and cautioned that she should never be underestimated. "She's a genius politician, but I don't know if she has that same affable charm that her husband does. But then, who does?'"

Donald Trump felt that Hillary Clinton moved to the left, referring to their promises of spending on programs such as higher education and paid family leave. "She wants to compete with Senator Bernie Sanders. Hillary and Bernie Sanders could not give away things fast enough, and worst of all they're giving them to illegal immigrants. Health care is for illegal immigrants. Driver licenses are for illegal immigrants. They want social security for illegal immigrants." Trump calls Bernie Sanders a maniac and a communist/socialist.

JEB BUSH

The Bush family is prominent in politics. With many members who have been successful bankers and businessmen, the family has two U.S. Senators, one Supreme Court Justice, two Governors and two Presidents. George Walker Bush and Barbara Bush have been married for 70 years.

In February 2015, a significant incident arose that should have made front-page news but did not. It involves Charles Koch, David Koch, and Jeb Bush in a deal that allowed Koch Industries and Georgia Pacific to dump millions of gallons of toxic waste on a daily basis for almost ten years into the St. John's River in Florida without the public's knowledge. The residents of Florida were not informed or aware of this corrupt deal between the Koch brothers and the Governors.

Jeb Bush is trying to establish the Bush brand in the Republican Party. The former Florida governor cracks the list of Republican presidential prospects that Charles and David Koch, and GOP mega-donors are considering in 2016.

Charles Koch said he and his brother have identified five likely hopefuls whose message they like and who have a chance.

Bush is on that list with Scott Walker Ted Cruz, Rand Paul and Marco Rubio.

Bush's campaign is changing the way they run their presidential races. Bush wants to outsource key tasks, including television ads and direct mail, to a super PAC, which can raise unlimited cash, instead of joining the official Bush campaign.

Bush try to keep his head down and raise as much money as possible in an effort to muscle out Trump, hire a talented staff and build a campaign that can compete against Clinton in 2016.

Bush attended the California forum organized by the Koch Brothers fundraising network, unlike his brother who reaches it from the back doors. Jeff Bush playing it safe, while opting to make his opinions known on Facebook and twitter, rather than on television. Republicans are familiar with the moves Bush is making. **At an event Jeb Bush made a radical statement that it was time to seriously consider "phasing out" Medicare.** Bush's talking points are as untrue and unpopular. Donald Trump was not discussed at the event and the Kochs appeared dismissive when Jeb Bush's name came up. The Koch Brothers have also warmed up to Carly Fiorina. Slowly but surely the Koch brothers big money is switching to Marco Rubio. Charles and David Koch will throw nearly $1 billion contribution behind him.

Meanwhile Trump and Bush are playing cat and mouse.

"El hombre no es conservador," Bush said in Spanish of Trump in Miami. That means that Bush is saying of Trump: "The man is not conservative."

"I like Jeb," Trump said. "He's a nice man. But he should really set the example by speaking English while in the United States."

Trump ripped that argument of him not being a conservative.

"You know, Ronald Reagan wasn't a conservative," Trump said. "He became a great conservative. By the time I am finished, people will say I am a great conservative. By the time I'm finished with the Presidency, after eight years of the Presidency, people will say I'm a great conservative, far greater than Jeb would ever have the ability to be."

In another occasion, Trump criticized Bush for planting a mole in his campaign and trying to sabotage his campaign.

During an appearance at a Jon Huntsman "No Labels" event, a female audience member named Lauren Batchelder played the role of antagonist female toward Trump.

However, Ms. Batchelder is not just an average audience member. She is a paid political operative of the GOP and a paid staff member of Team Jeb Bush:

In contrast, of Senator Ayotte's position, being pro-life, it didn't take long to figure out this was a planted GOP hit job, targeting Donald Trump:

Batchelder quickly began scrubbing her social media history trying to hide whom she works for. Almost all of her Twitter history was deleted, but not before much of it was able to be captured.

"How can Jeb Bush expect to deal with China, Russia + Iran if he gets caught doing a 'plant' during my speech yesterday in NH?" Trump added.

The Bush campaign admitted that the female audience member, identified by a conservative website as Lauren Batchelder, volunteered at events in New Hampshire for the former Florida governor but denied the accusation that she was a plant, saying Batchelder spoke for herself and that her question was not sanctioned by the campaign.

The feud between Donald Trump and Jeb Bush over the Sept. 11 terrorist attacks escalated as Trump argued that his hard-liner stand on immigration would have prevented the attacks; while Bush try to defend his brother George W., Trump insists he is not blaming the former President for Sept. 11.

"I'm not blaming anybody, but the World Trade Center came down, so when he said we were safe, we were not safe. We lost 3,000 people. It was probably the greatest catastrophe ever in this country," Trump said.

"George W. Bush was president, OK? Blame him or don't blame him, but he was the President. And the World Trade Center came down during his reign," Trump added.

* * * * *

Jeb Bush has built a formidable campaign with top staff in all the early states and announced a respectable third-quarter haul of $13.4 million, which only 5% of it came from small donations. That proves that $12 million of the money came from influential donors.

Bush has struggled to get attention in the shadow of Trump.

Bush raised more money in the third quarter than rival Marco Rubio. His campaign is spending carefully to avoid running out of money.

On the other side, Trump is stripping Jeff Bush out of the donor's money, leaving him in despair.

MARCO RUBIO

Trump called Rubio "a kid who shouldn't even be running for President, adding that his foreign policies are better than Rubio's. Rubio fired back, calling Trump "touchy and insincere."

Trump had harsh words for Marco Rubio for aiming to undercut his campaign slogan, "Make America Great Again." Ronald Reagan used the campaign slogan in the 1980 campaign for the White House alongside Jeb's father, George Bush. Rubio said that Trump's campaign slogan is not an accurate assessment of the country. Rubio argued America is "great" now.

Trump, in response, said this means Rubio is satisfied with where America is now, and does not believe there is room for improvement. Trump also called Rubio "Jeb's plebe."

Trump said that to be elected presidential candidates have to talk about their foreign policy. He commented that Marco Rubio has the worst voting record and that his sweat glands are overactive. Trump said that he knows more about Syria than the Senate Foreign Policy Committee member Marco Rubio.

"The Syrian dictator Bashar Assad, is saying, 'I can't believe it, Americans are killing my enemy, this is the greatest thing happening to me.' Marco Rubio wants to tell every single thing that he knows to everybody, so that the people on the other side, so that the enemy can learn all about it. I want to be unpredictable to them." Trump said.

Trump's presidential campaign continued escalating the feud with Marco Rubio. But, despite the back-and-forth jabs between the two candidates lately, Trump advisor, Michael Cohen, insists that Rubio "doesn't mean anything to Trump."

"Trump doesn't want to pick a fight, but if you pick a fight with him, you're doomed to lose," Cohen said. "Trump doesn't think about Marco Rubio, Marco Rubio means nothing to him. And as far as foreign policy, what gives

Marco Rubio the right to talk about foreign policy?"

So, Trump called Rubio a "clown" a remark that was not well received by the conservative audience, many of them began to cheer Trump.

Bush trained Rubio in Florida politics before the two, along with 15 other Republicans, started competing against each other for the GOP nomination. Rubio and Bush have nearly identical political viewpoints on immigration and trade, as Bush and his campaign keeps slipping more and more. It is expected that the donor paymasters will get behind Rubio down the road, because he would give them everything they want if he is elected President, just as Bush would.

Trump thinks that no matter who the establishment puts forward, whether it be Bush, Rubio, or John Kasich, "they are all controlled" by the paymasters who are funding their campaigns. Without naming names, Trump revealed. "They are controlling the politicians. I used to be one of those people, at the highest level. I was one of them," Trump said. "Nobody knows the game better than I do. I think part of the reason I am resonating with the public is that I do not want money. I just hope the public appreciates what I'm doing. The donor's paymasters are controlling politicians like Bush and Rubio. They are looking to benefit themselves or their company, whereas I am looking only to benefit the people of the United States."

Trump attacks Rubio's attendance record in the Senate, his work on comprehensive immigration reform and his financial controversies.

SEN. TED CRUZ

The Texas GOP senator has praised Trump for drawing attention to illegal immigration, and headlined a rally with him against President Barack Obama's nuclear deal with Iran and repeatedly passed on opportunities to attack him in public.

However, Ted Cruz is not stupid. He is cozying up to Donald Trump in a cynical ploy to court the billionaire supporters should Trump drop out of the race. Cruz has made no bones about looking to lure Trump supporters, reiterating he is working for the support of every voter, even those already aligned with other candidates.

Ted Cruz said that he not only believes he can beat front-runner Donald Trump, but trump's supporters will end up voting for him instead.

"I don't believe Donald is going to be the nominee and I think in time the lion's share of his supporters end up with us," the senator said.

Trump will be wise not to be close to Ted Cruz. He may turn deadly in the end.

The Louisiana governor Jindal has been the only one to allege that Cruz is "clinging to Trump like a limpet to an oil tanker, hoping to suck up his votes if Trump eventually sinks. Jindal has been polling near the bottom of national surveys, and his full-throated attacks on Trump, have been viewed as an attempt to breathe new life into his campaign giving him a fresh round of attention since a recent poll showed him pulling further down.

JOHN BOEHNER

Trump suggested that Boehner and other members of the Republican establishment in Congress do not have the courage to stand up and fight for what they want, regardless of whether it causes a government shutdown. Americans would blame it on President Obama, not on Republican lawmakers.

"I think it's time," Trump said "These people, they're babies. I think the Republican establishment has not gotten the job done, there are tremendous problems. I'm not surprised to see it. A lot of people thought it was going to happen earlier."

Trump's comments that he wasn't surprised—because of Boehner's failures and lack of leadership.

"It's going to be very telling who gets it," Trump said of the future Speaker. "It's going to be very competitive, and I don't think it's going to go to any one particular person. But whoever gets that position, it's going to be very telling about what happens in the future."

MITCH MCCONNELL

In the wake of Speaker John Boehner's impending retirement, some on the right have said the Senate majority leader should also leave Congress.

However, Trump said he likes McConnell. Even though he does not know him well, but he would like to see, the Senate run in a "tougher" manner.

A top Republican Chairman Roger Villere has called for Senate Majority Leader Sen. Mitch McConnell's resignation. Now that the Republican base has focused on Mitch McConnell, their attention could spell trouble for Marco Rubio. The Senator risked his political career by advancing the goals of Mitch McConnell, casting the 60th and deciding vote for Obama trade, and namely co-author of the Gang of Eight Amnesty Bill.

Although the Republican base overwhelmingly opposed the policies in Rubio's Amnesty Bill, Mitch McConnell refused to block the bill from coming up to a vote.

Although McConnell eventually cast his vote against the Gang of Eight Bill, he did so only after it was clear that the bill would pass the Senate, and after he had done everything that was necessary to ensure its smooth passage.

Only days before Boehner's resignation announcement, Rubio seemed to defend John Boehner and Mitch McConnell, arguing that Republican voters were expecting too much when they sent their elected officials to Washington.

"The idea that you would win the Senate, control the agenda never was true," he said. "You need a President. It's one of the main reasons why I decided to run for President."

From the Oval Office, Rubio would have a much greater vantage point to enact Mitch McConnell's agenda and increase the admission of foreign workers.

Given the strong desire of Republican voters to remove Mitch McConnell, it remains to be seen whether the voters will be willing to give over control of the Republican Party to the young Rubio who has been the most ever faithful champion of McConnell.

MEGYN KELLY

Fox News Channel's Megyn Kelly admitted there were difficult aspects in dealing with the controversy on her on-and-off controversy with Donald Trump. Kelly thought she would make a bigger name for herself by trumping the Trump, and instead helped power his new numbers-busting popularity. It was another defeat for the press.

Fox News CEO Roger Ailes wanted to confer on what was happening on his end. He was hearing from Trump a lot. She clarified she was counseled by him. She has repeatedly been in the news since the debate — and it's all due to Donald Trump.

Kelly was slammed by Trump for her "ridiculous" and "off-base" questions about misogynistic comments he has made in the past, including calling women "fat pigs," "dogs," "slobs," and "disgusting animals."

Trump, who made no secret of his contempt for Kelly, told Don Lemon that during the debate, "You could see there was blood coming out of her eyes, blood coming out of her...wherever."

That comment sparked a swift backlash from Republicans and Democrats alike that saw an opportunity to get rid of Trump who is gaining support and winning the battle in the race.

But Trump continued to attack Kelly on social media and news shows, mocking her and questioning her professionalism. Some of his supporters also began targeting Kelly on social media.

Kelly responded because Fox News CEO Roger Ailes pressed her for comment. The real issue is that NBC and Trump began a battle because NBC's policies are inclined to not support the Conservative point of view, and more likely to corroborate the left wing policies. Many of NBC encores are actually siding with the Democrat's VIEW politically for years, and Kelly is one of them.

FOX NEWS

Donald Trump, front-runner for the Republican Presidential Nomination, steam-rolled a new poll showing his lead growing.

Donald Trump plays with the Koch brothers and they have tried numerous times to put him on the strings and break him down. No one ever went against the Koch brothers, and that means going against Fox News. Trump knows where the real battle is and has successfully beaten the Koch brothers, time after time. Democrats have been waiting for years to tell everyone this dirty secret.

Trump has zero filters and it will be fun to watch him turn the weapon onto his own kind. He will tell everything! He knows how they work with their bathroom deals. When they try to push him out, he will take them down with him. He's a bully and they can't put him back in the box. 'Tear them up for us, Trump.' They scream.

On another footnote, Trump went on to trash Charles Krauthammer, Megyn Kelly, and Rich Lowry.

"I think various things happened. I mean, it has to do with polling too. They do not put up the good polls. They do not put up polls. If I'm leading big in a poll, they don't put it up. All of them have been so wrong, and the level of hatred and animosity is incredible." Trump said.

Trump calls the editor a 'dope' After Fox contributor Rich Lowry commented on Donald Trump's performance at the last GOP debate, Trump says Lowry is a 'dope' and a 'loser'.

Since 2012, the big three networks have reported on the Koch brothers and their funding of political campaigns 9 times more often than liberal billionaires George Soros and Tom Steyer.

ABC, CBS and NBC have entirely ignored big money liberal organizations like the Democracy Alliance, which is spending $200 million to "boost liberal candidates and causes."

These networks dug up professional left-wingers like host Stephen Colbert and Chris Matthews of MSNBC, to whine about conservative money. Most of the traditional news outlets ignore the conservative comments about liberal funding. However, when the lefties whine about a conservative funder, the media outlets rush to help.

Journalists did everything but peep through keyholes tracking the Kochs. Liberal funders, on the other hand, could literally throw cash at their candidates and the media looks the other way.

So you see, this not about Trump and NBC or Magen Kelly, It's all about who controls the politicians and the media.

THE MEXICAN BORDER

When it comes to the border, Trump noted that he would build a wall if elected President.

"I know this: We need a wall, and we need it badly," Trump said, "And it's got to be an impenetrable wall. We're taking in people legally, but we're not taking in any more illegals, but we will take them in legally."

When asked what he would do about the more than 11 million immigrants already living in the U.S. illegally he said. "We're rounding them up in a very humane way, in a very nice way. I know it doesn't sound nice. But not everything is nice. It is practical. It's going to work. They have to come here legally. And you know, when I talk about the wall, and I said it before, we're going to have a tremendous, beautiful, wide-open door. We want people to come into the country."

Immigration continues to be the issue that will largely define his candidacy, though he was surprised at the strength of the response he has gotten about the Mexican border.

"I had no idea it was going to resonate in the way it has," he said.

He also called on revisions to immigration laws to fight the whole anchor baby situation, which is insane, referring to laws that allow immigrants who give birth in the United States to stay in the country.

"I want people to come into the country, but I want them to come in legally," Trump said.

TRUMP'S HEALTHCARE

Trump pushed back against Republicans who have attacked him for supporting a single-payer healthcare system in the past.

He said he would release formal details on his healthcare plan soon.

"People think this is not traditionally Republican, but I think it is because I don't want to see people dying on the streets and neither do other Republicans want to see that," Trump said. "I'm not a conservative that wants to take care of 60 percent of the people and let the other 40 percent rot in hell. That is not going to be me. You can't do that and I don't think most Republicans want to do that either."

Specifically, he said his plan would break down inter-state barriers that prevent people from going across state lines to purchase healthcare plans, a plan championed by many other conservatives.

But his rivals have seized on his evolving position about the exact role he thinks government should play in the healthcare system.

Trump articulates that much of his plan will come out of the pockets of insurance companies, which he says are thriving under Obamacare.

TRUMP ON IRAN DEAL

"Never, ever in my life, have I seen any transaction so incompetently negotiated as our deal with Iran," Trump said. "And I mean never."

Unlike most of his rivals for the Republican Presidential Nomination, Donald Trump would not rescind President Barack Obama's nuclear deal with Iran.

Republican presidential candidates have promised to rip up the deal on the first day of their presidency. Trump argued that it would be unrealistic to do so because it would be hard to recoup the $150 billion Iran would gain.

He promised to "police" Iran to make sure the country does not break the terms of the agreement.

"The problem is by the time I got in there, they will have already received the $150 billion," he said. "Do you know if the deal gets rejected they still get the money? I couldn't believe it. If the deal is rejected, they still get all of this money. Iran is going to be unbelievably powerful and unbelievably rich."

Trump is not running in the Republican Party like others. He is running as someone who can think out of the box and his followers love him for that. He is forcing others to prove why the ripping up the deal on day one is a better option. He is paying his own way.

Trump brings attention to the four hostages being held in the Islamic country, including Christian pastor Saeed Abedini.

"If I win the Presidency I guarantee you that those four prisoners are back in our country before I ever take office. They know it and if they don't know it, I'm telling them right now."

Trump addressed Iran's Ayatollah, who declared that Israel would not survive the next 25 years.

"Our president is calling the person who is really the boss in Iran a 'Supreme Leader,'" Trump said. "It just came out a little while ago, he said Israel will not exist in 25 years...He also said very strongly that this is the end of our dealings with the United States...So, they rip us off, they take our money, they make us look like fools, and now they're back to being who they are. They don't want Israel to survive...with incompetent leadership like we have right now, Israel will NOT survive. We are led by very stupid people. We cannot let it continue."

"We lose everywhere," Trump added. "We lose militarily. We can't beat ISIS. Give me a break...We will have so much winning if I get elected you might get bored with winning."

"We're going to have such a strong military that nobody is going to mess with us. We're not going to have to use it," Trump concluded.

"We're going to make America great again."

ON TAXES & ECONOMY

Trump revealed a tax plan that will generate rapid economic growth.

People should be able to keep more money in their pockets after-tax. Simplifying the tax code let everyone keep more of their money.

If you are single and earn less than $25,000, or married and jointly earn less than $50,000, you will not owe any income tax. That removes nearly 75 million households. They get a new one-page form to send the IRS saying, "I win."

All other Americans will get a simpler tax code with four brackets instead of seven.

Businesses will pay in taxes no more than 15% of their business income. This lower rate makes corporate inversions unnecessary by making America's tax rate one of the best in the world.

No family will have to pay the death tax. You earned and saved that money for your family.

The Trump plan eliminates the income tax for over 73 million households.

Those within the 10% bracket will keep all or most of their current deductions. Those within the 20% bracket will keep more than half of their current deductions. Those within the 25% bracket will keep fewer deductions. Charitable giving and mortgage interest deductions will remain unchanged for all taxpayers. it will boost consumer spending, and maximize economic growth.

Corporations will no longer be allowed to defer taxes on income earned abroad, but the foreign tax credit will remain in place because no company should face double taxation.

Trump's proposal cuts the top individual tax rate to 25 percent, and the corporate tax rate to 15 percent, and would eliminate the Estate Tax. The largest share of tax break benefits will be provided to the upper income earners. To address the trillions of dollars in lost revenue, Trump said his plan could boost economic growth as high as 6 percent.

"We're going to have growth that will be tremendous,"

Trump released a tax plan that proposed slashing income taxes for Americans across the board.

One measure in Trump's tax proposal aimed at bringing in

revenue is the abolishment of the so-called "carried interest" loophole. That would tax the profits for some investors like hedge fund managers at a higher rate. Trump acknowledged that closing the carried interest loophole is not enough, but an important psychological thing to do.

The Democrats insist that Dodd-Frank controls Wall Street and will prevent the economy from collapsing by giving regulators the power they need to oversight the process. Republicans criticize the law as retaliatory to small businesses.

Donald Trump believes the Democrats, as well as the Federal Reserve manipulation of the interest rates about to burst, due to The Dodd-Frank Act, the financial reform package, create the stock market bubble. America needs to be on alert.

"The regulators are running the banks," Trump said. "The bankers are petrified of regulators. And the problem is that the banks aren't loaning money to people who create jobs."

Right now, the Retail industries' sales, account for two thirds of economic activity, and they are falling. Corporate profits are plunging. The Wall Street people refuse to acknowledge recession reality.

Trump also slammed Federal Reserve Chief Janet Yellen for artificially suppressing interest rates for political reasons, because President Obama does not want to have a depression during his administration. The last two employment reports were bad.

"The Fed never took their foot off the gas, so we are headed for the cliff at 100 miles per hour. I wonder what happens next."

TRUMP ON SYRIA

Vladimir Putin is clever, confident in his command of information, at times droll, and sometimes adamant.

He positioned himself as a friend of world stability. Russia is in Syria to keep it from becoming what Libya is, a nation in which "all the state institutions are disintegrated." The Syrian government of Bashar Assad has "the one legitimate conventional army," and "I want you and your audience to finally realize that no one except for the Assad army is fighting ISIS and other terrorist groups now in Syria. It has to be said frankly this is a very low level of effectiveness. I'm not trying to be sarcastic here. I'm not trying to call someone out or to point fingers."

Putin sees ISIS as a unique terrorist organization. "I'm trying to prevent a vacuum where the government of Syria should be. Right now it's filled with terrorists."

As the United States confronts the threat of ISIS, Trump weighed in on the disagreement between President Barack Obama and Vladimir Putin on the best approach to take with Syrian President Bashar al-Assad.

"Let Russia fight ISIS if they want to fight them," he said. "Russia likes Assad seemingly a lot. Let them worry about ISIS. Let them fight it-out. Some of the candidates want to start World War III over Syria," Trump said. "If we're going to have World War III, it's not going to be over Syria. I won't even call them hawks. I call them fools." Trump said.

PEGGY NOONAN

Peggy Noonan had a column in the WSJ about Donald Trump. She resides in north Georgia near the Tennessee line she is in her 60s, and lives on Social Security. In 2012, she voted Republican, after she was disappointed in Mr. Obama who could not make anything work or get anything done.

Peggy Noonan declared that the country would be in much better shape with Trump as President. He is very wealthy and can turn around the economy. "He will get things moving and will kick ass." She said the Army soldiers are completely disgusted and furious, and Trump is igniting their passion. "He's telling them 'I will make this country great again,' and they believe him."

And ISIS won't like it that he's in charge.

Trump strikes her as a serious man, and a patriot. "All he does is talk about how great this country is and how greater he can make it, how he wants to get good trade deals and take care of veterans. He does not need this job, he already has everything, it's a pay cut. He does not need the stature. I think he wants the job because he wants to do it."

He is concerned about what everyone is concerned about, except politicians. "The biggest problem is all the illegal immigrants."

Peggy Noonan states, "It doesn't bother me that he is not a professional politician, and it doesn't bother the American people. And if you asked the people down South here, they don't care either. They just want somebody in whose plain and simple, can get the job done." Otherwise, she worries, "we're going to be Greece in another four, five years."

"We need a very tough businessman with great business shrewdness. We can restore the highways, tunnels, and airports, and he will rebuild them. He will build a wall with Mexico. If he gets it done that's fine."

"He comes across as self-made. In spite of his wealth, he never made himself smooth, polite. He is like someone you know. This is part of his power."

"Donald knew the political machine and its players and went

on to give political donations based on power, not party. Yet his supporters experience him as outside the system, unsullied by it. He is a practical man who did what practical men have to do. His rise is not due to his supporters' anger at government. It is a gesture of contempt for government, for the men and women in Congress, the White House, and the agencies. It is precisely because people have lost their awe for the Presidency that they imagine Mr. Trump as a viable President."

American political establishment, take note: In the past 20 years you have turned America into a third world nation and people would make Donald Trump their president.

Trump supporters likes that he does not in the least fear the press, does not get the dart-eyed, anxious look candidates get. He treats reporters with courtesy until he feels they are out of line, at which point he calls them stupid. They think he will do that with Putin. His insult of John McCain did not hurt him, and not because his supporters have any animus for Mr. McCain. They just saw it, as more proof Mr. Trump will take the bark off anyone.

Trump can call any TV show and instantly is put through to the anchor. No other candidate, from either party, is given that luxury, but then no other candidate's mere presence results in an immediate spike in viewers.

"You cannot turn on the TV without seeing Donald Trump," says Kevin Madden, a senior adviser to both of Mitt Romney's presidential campaigns, "It is nearly impossible not to be at or near the top of the polls when you get that much attention."

Trump declares the Iran nuclear deal "will lead to a nuclear holocaust", but would seek to implement it nonetheless, and says he would send troops back into Iraq to secure oil fields seized by Islamic state fighters.

"You go and knock the hell out of the oil, take back the oil," he says. "We're going to have so much money." The Iraqi people will get "something", he adds, but "we should definitely take back money for our soldiers".

To understand Trump philosophy you have to compare him to Ronald Reagan. Reagan had a defined political outlook that shaped his Presidency and influenced his party, agree or not.

Reagan saw government as a beast that needed to be subdued and shrunken.

Trump said in his announcement speech. "Save Medicare, Medicaid and Social Security without cuts, we have to do it, Get rid of the fraud. Get rid of the waste and abuse but save it. People have been paying it for years."

* * * * *

Trump has been the Republican front-runner, solidly leading his GOP rivals in Florida, Ohio and Pennsylvania.

What will it be to have a party establishment try to 'kill' the guy whose No. 1 in that party's polls? Maybe they think they will have excellent opposition, but opposition does not really work on Trump, mostly because his supporters do not think he is a sweet, sinless businessman. They love it that he is not. More candidates will drop out, as voters will begin to conjoin behind the front-runners. The GOP apparatus is going to use every trick they have deployed in the past to stop Donald Trump from winning the nomination.

THE VETERANS

At least 40 U.S. veterans died waiting for appointments at the Phoenix Veterans Affairs Health Care system, many of whom were placed on a secret waiting list.

The secret list was part of an elaborate scheme designed by Veterans Affairs managers in Phoenix who were trying to hide those 1,400 to 1,600 sick veterans forced into long waiting periods to see a doctor, according to a recently retired top VA doctor and several high-level sources.

Two hundred and fifty thousand veterans put on a VA death list in past years are refused care. Forty thousand active troops are going to receive layoff notices over the next four years and enter the VA list. The Government did not address their health issues, which many resulted in death.

Trump was threatening to pull out of the CNN debate if they did not give the additional advertising revenue that they would be earning to charity. CNN did not agree with his demand to donate the money from the ad revenue to the veterans. Trump said he would make a determination whether to show to the debate.

CNN was charging $5,000 a minute. With the anticipated audience for the September 16th debate, CNN's charging $200,000 a minute.

In the last few months, in order to hide how many people have died while waiting for care at the Phoenix VA hospital, the records were changed or physically altered, even in recent weeks. To make statistics look better, those veterans were not counted as having died while in care.

The alterations occurred in deliberate attempts to hide how many veterans died while waiting for care, by trying to pretend dead veterans remain alive.

That created a national fury that prompted Senate hearings and ultimately led to the resignation of President Obama's VA Secretary, Eric Shinseki.

The VA's Office of Inspector General also has investigators in 69 other locations, looking into charges of other data manipulation, delays and deaths, and retaliation allegations of whistle-blower.

The Obama administration's Veterans Affairs (VA) scandal, left veterans dying while the government they served denied them medical care. Trump has made veterans' care a major talking point in his stump speeches, charging that illegal immigrants receive better care than the nations wounded soldiers do, Trump vowed to offer frustrated veterans subsidized private health care.

CHINA

Donald Trump has been reminding Americans to be concerned about North Korea's nuclear weapon program. Trump said

"I would do something. You have to do something about North Korea. Now what I would do is, I would make China respect us because China has extreme control over North Korea. And I would say, "China, you better go in there and you better do something because economically it could cost China."

Trump talks about China because it allows him to argue that China constantly beats the United States in trade deals. The largest bank in the world has offices in Trump Tower.

Alongside Mexico, Trump's speeches frequently mention how the U.S. is losing to China's leaders who are outsmarting Washington on economic issues. Despite his steady stream of criticism aimed at the country, Trump is not getting under China's skin.

Trump is getting tough on China in foreign policy, including putting tariffs on goods produced overseas. We owe China $1.3 trillion. Trump said that trades with China are "the greatest transfer of wealth in history."

When Trump speaks about Chinese theft, he is talking about intellectual property. The Chinese stock market experienced a huge decline and gave the Chinese government a reason to devalue its own currency by stating it will help its own economy. Trump remarks that it was a deliberate act against the USA.

Donald Trump said that China's devaluation of the yuan would be "devastating" for the United States as the global currency war enters a new and critical phase.

"They're just destroying us," Trump said, a long-time critic of China's currency policy.

They're doing a big cut in the yuan, and that's going to be devastating for us."

The yuan devaluation puts the Fed in a difficult spot. It opens the possibility that the Fed should not delay a rate increase.

Over the past decade, the U.S. Congress has pressed Beijing to loosen its dollar-pegged exchange rate to allow the yuan to appreciate; arguing that a trillion dollars of currency market intervention depressed the yuan artificially, and gave China an unfair trade advantage in global export markets.

That made sense with China growing 10 percent per annum and attracting hundreds of billions of dollars of global capital every year.

The People's Bank of China described its move, which caught markets by surprise, as a depreciation of the yuan as a free-market reform.

"If China is really moving towards greater alignment with the market, which implies greater yuan weakness, this may be a factor that adds more pressure on China-related currencies," says a Barclays Asia-based strategist in a note to the public.

Many emerging market currencies, including the Malaysian ringgit, Indonesian Rupiah and Brazil's Real, had already slumped to their weakest levels against the dollar in over a decade as capital fled their slowing economies.

The big question now for the Asian markets and Emerging markets is whether their officials respond to China.

Nick Lawson, managing director at Deutsche Bank in London said, "There should be further pressure on the currencies of China's trade partners," said.

Central banks dumped as much as $260 billion of foreign exchange reserves in the second quarter as emerging market central banks tried to mitigate the impact of capital fleeing their own economies.

THE SECRET SERVICE

Obama was given Secret Service protection on May 3, 2007. At the time, law enforcement officials acknowledged it was unusually early in the presidential cycle to grant a presidential candidate protection, but also said it was not based on specific threats.

Donald Trump demanded the Secret Service should be giving him protection, and he suggested that partisan politics might be behind the agency decision not to provide it.

Trump pointed out that he has attracted large crowds just like Barack Obama did eight years ago as a White House candidate by this point in the 2008 cycle, the Illinois senator had the Secret Service protection.

"I want to put them on notice because they should have a liability," he said. "Personally, I think if Obama were doing as well as me he would've had Secret Service."

The Department of Homeland Security said they had not received an official request for protection from Trump.

"If a request is received, a determination of Secret Service protection would be made after a consultation with an advisory committee including House and Senate leaders from both parties."

Trump praises his private security team, but says people have expressed concern to him about his safety.

Trump's move was to put the Secret Service 'on notice.'

The Secret Service is extending protection to GOP presidential contenders Donald Trump and Ben Carson.

Trump and Carson will receive agents, with each candidate assigned approximately two dozen agents.

REPUBLICAN PRESIDENTIAL CANDIDATES

Chris Christie

Chris Christie tells it like it is and does not care whom he offends – even when he gets in trouble for being nice. More than a few people on all sides have surely used his portrait as a dartboard, but he has earned a lot of respect for his fearless tongue, and Republicans appreciate his conservative ideology.

Dr. Ben Carson

Ben Carson is a highly accomplished physician who is seen as a breath of fresh air in the world of politics. He has left his position as Director of Pediatric Neurosurgery at Johns Hopkins Medical Center, and since then he is in pursuit of the U.S. presidency in 2016.

Marco Rubio

Marco Rubio is definitely on the short list of names for Republican frontrunner. Being himself of Cuban heritage, he enjoys strong support among the important Latino demographic, in addition to holding solid conservative principles that make him eminently likeable to the Republican constituency.

Rick Santorum

The former two-term Senator from Pennsylvania announced yet another bid to be the party's nominee for President in 2016 on May 27, 2015. With a small but loyal base behind him, Senator Santorum will work to expand his demographic appeal over the next months.

Carly Fiorina

The only well-known woman running for the Republican nomination in 2016, Carly Fiorina is a unique political figure. Her business experience and conservative principles make her attractive to the right, but past difficulties and failures could haunt her moving forward.

Bobby Jindal

Gov. Jindal created history in 2008 when he became the first Indian American to be elected a state Governor. At the

grand old age of 24, the Rhodes Scholar was appointed by Gov. Murphy Foster to manage the Health and Human Services Dept., the largest department in the state.

Mike Huckabee

Mike Huckabee is an Evangelical Christian who never shy away from his faith. In January 2015, he bid farewell as host of his popular talk show on the Fox News Channel to pursue his 2016 presidential bid.

Rand Paul

Sen. Paul finally emerged from the huge shadow of his larger than life father, maverick Republican Ron Paul, when he was selected to deliver the tea party response to President Obama's SOTU address in 2013, and in the process, cementing his de facto leadership of the movement.

Lindsey Graham

The former Colonel with the USAF JAG unit has been one of the most recognized Republican faces in the post-2012 election era. However, his reputation as a compromise broker in Congress has taken a hit over his recent conversion into a foreign policy hawk.

Jeb Bush

Florida's only Republican two-term Governor, Jeb Bush is a heavyweight political contender who comes from a family of presidents. His left-leaning ideologies make him too liberal for the taste of some in his party, however, and his lineage could be a hindrance rather than help.

George Pataki

A three-term Governor of New York State with an impressive political career besides, George Pataki is a red Republican who has found success in blue country. His fiscal policies are pleasing enough to the GOP base, but his stance on social issues may leave something to be desired.

John Kasich

The sitting Governor of Ohio has enjoyed stunning political success over his life, and he's hoping to ride it all the way to the White House in 2016. His incomplete rejection of Obamacare has put him on the outs with the Tea Party, but other Republicans are likely to back his strong conservative policies.

There are still a lot more participants in this race.

WHAT IF

- If Trump will win the primaries, the Republicans will win the Presidency. He is Charismatic and ready for action. Resemble the Sun.

- If Ben Carson will win the primaries, the Republicans will lose the Presidency again. He has Charisma of a surfboard. Came out of nowhere.

- If Jeb Bush will win the primaries, the republican will lose again. America will fall asleep. He is too dry. Americans are afraid of another Bush rule over them. He is married to a Spanish woman. He speaks Spanish, so, what went wrong?

- If Bernie sanders will win the primaries, the Democrats will lose the presidency. The USA will merge with Russia and become a communist country.

- Fiorina returned to her normal size. Thank God.

- Marco the Cuban? Only thirsty individuals will vote for him. He will sell the Republican Party to the highest bidders.

- If Ted Cruz will win the primaries, the Republican will lose the Presidency. He does not have much of a chance. Under no circumstances is he able to compete with a charismatic and compelling candidate.

- If Hillary Clinton will win the primaries, the Republicans may lose the Presidency again. If she does not end up in Jail soon, she may find enough young and restless people to vote for her. Don't forget that Hillary has the charisma of city bus.

- If Ben Carson will win the primaries, the Republicans may lose the Presidency again. As soon as he opens his mouth, you realize that he is not the one we are looking for.

The End

Trump